# POSITIONAL PLAY
# Back Defenders

*by*
**Allen Wade**

*Published by*
REEDSWAIN INC

# Library of Congress Cataloging - in - Publication Data

Wade, Allen
 Positional Play - Back Defenders

ISBN No. 1-890946-10-9
Copyright © 1997 Allen Wade
Library of Congress Catalog Card Number 97-075737

Reedswain books are available at special discounts for bulk purchase. For details contact the Special Sales Manager at Reedswain 1-800-331-5191.

Credits: Art Direction, Layout, Design and Diagrams • Kimberly N. Bender
Cover Photo: Empics

## REEDSWAIN VIDEOS AND BOOKS, INC.
612 Pughtown Road • Spring City Pennsylvania 19475
1-800-331-5191

# Table of Contents

# Chapter 1
# The Full-Backs' Role in Team Play

In the early days of systematic team play there were four 'lines' in the formations adopted by most teams. Forwards, usually two wide attackers (wingers) and a centre forward were the principle goal scorers. Inside forwards, the play controllers, operated behind the front 'line'. Behind the inside forwards were their 'minders', two wing half-backs so named because, in the very earliest days of team tactics, they marked opposing wingers and were stationed half way towards the backs. The back line was formed by the full-backs, initially two, soon reinforced by a third and in recent times by a fourth and occasionally a fifth.

In England two of the backs became known as wide or wing backs, one or two others as the centre backs and one as the libero or sweeper centre back. The libero has a free covering role behind the other backs and also, in positive teams, has license to move forward into attacking involvements. Nevertheless English tradition causes a central back to be known as the centre half back even though in reality he is a centre full-back! There goes our Irish ancestry again, as if the language itself doesn't produce enough problems.

The different alignments of and the numerical bias towards the backs have reflected the importance attached to the avoidance of defeat in professional soccer. The English may have a word for it but hardly any teams in English professional soccer have shown the wit needed to adopt the role or to understand the opportunities presented by using the 'libero' system. Consequently they are not too successful at defeating the tactic.

I am in a small minority, in the game's mother country, who believe that adopting and adapting the sweeper system is the essential pre-condition to any serious attempt to resurrect England's position in world soccer. The rest of the world simply cannot have been wrong.

Nowadays, systematic soccer has been based upon three 'line' deployments involving backs, mid-field players and strikers (forwards). These groups, or lines vary greatly in numbers producing the team systems so beloved of journalists and so easily, if simplistically, described as 1/4-3-3, 1/4-4-2, 1/4-5-1, 1/1-3-3-3 and so on; the first one being the goalkeeper. Not only do the numbers of players deployed forward, in mid-field and at the back vary from team to team, in outstanding teams they are highly fluid even during the course of any single match.

Wherever distinct lines of players forming an unchanging pattern are seen during a match, and especially when those lines are made up of the same players occupying the same positions relative to each other, the game is certain to be predictable, static and unimaginative. Teams adopting rigid playing systems do so hoping that organization alone will induce errors in their opponents' play. It will not!

Success, at the top level, is based upon a team's capacity to present rapidly changing, fluid problems to their opponents. Fluid systems of play demand players who are capable of playing competently in all team positions and outstandingly in one or two. Rigid systems produce limited players who are restricted in their skills and even more so in their imaginations.

## There's a limited soccer future for limited players.

Today, the role of the back has changed and is changing. The traditional area from which and through which teams developed attacking moves was mid-field; all very well when teams played to win by scoring as many goals as possible. Teams were prepared to attack by sending three, four or even five players forward prompted from behind by two or three more. The space in mid-field enabled both teams to test each other's skill in those areas and teams were happy to attack in turn and win with scores of 6-4 or 5-3 or even 4-1. Goal scoring was the game's objective.

As caution came to prevail, team strategies were devised to stop goals being scored rather than scoring them. Teams didn't play to win (by scoring goals); they played to avoid losing.

Mid-field became full of players. Controlled, clever possession and distribution of the ball in that area became impossible. In effect eighteen or often all twenty outfield players played the game using only one sixth of the pitch area available. That sixth moved towards one 'end' or the other as teams attacked or defended. Twenty top class athletes trying to play skillfully in about 1,500 square yards of pitch affords any individual little space or time in which to be skillful.

Without composure and control when in possession of the ball, without the perception needed to see and create clever, deceptive passing options, skillful interplay becomes impossible. Control, accuracy, cleverness and perception all require time. Soccer strategies and tactics, at the highest levels for many years, were specifically aimed at denying players time in which to be skillful. Consequently the top teams changed their tactics to establish controlled ball possession among the backs who set up counter attacking movements either through or over the congestion in mid-field. Defending teams were and still are reluctant to push strikers and midfield players forward in sufficient numbers to oppose controlled interpassing by the backs on a player to player basis. Two strikers are expected to contain three, four, even occasionally five opposing backs with the ball while larger groups of mid-field players deny opponents space and time behind them. Forwards, required to be effective 'first' defenders, predictably lost their capabilities for cleverly creating and taking scoring opportunities.

Pressuring opponents all over the field, full pressing as it is called, has not found favor among the world's top soccer coaches. . . yet. It will!

Back-field build up of attacking play has given the back a more balanced role. He must still be able to defend sternly by marking tightly, covering quickly and by intercepting and tackling surely. Additionally, he must be creative rather than exclusively destructive.

The need for control together with passing vision and 'touch' demand a different style of player, an all-rounder capable of playing well in all phases of play. The back's role, in modern soccer, is as much that of play-maker as of play-breaker.

Consideration of the back's role leads logically to the attributes upon which his successful development depends. They will be much the same for all backs, wide or central, with the exception of the 'libero'. His attributes and responsibilities will be dealt with separately.

# Chapter 2
# The Attributes of a Modern Full-Back

A ssuming that he has good basic technique and can play the game up to the required standard, I would look for the following qualities in a potentially outstanding full-back.

### 2.1 Tough mindedness.

All outstanding soccer players. . . and basketball players. . . and tennis players. . . and. . . pretty well all sports people at the top. . . must be tough minded: tough-mindedness must not be confused with tough play. Tough play, as interpreted by some coaches and players involves physically intimidating, violent or even foul play: in other words cheating. Genuinely tough minded players have no need to cheat; they take the greatest possible pleasure in beating anyone and everyone fairly, whatever their style of play. Tough-mindedness is the quality of never giving in mentally however severe the competition or however lost the cause may seem to be.

Percy Cerutty, a great Australian athletics coach, was overwhelmed by parents bringing youngsters to him in the expectation that he could turn them into world beaters at any event from 100 meters to the marathon. With laconic indifference to the eulogies of the kids' parents, he would tell them to run some extraordinary distance. . . fifteen or twenty miles say. He did so to eliminate those whose ambitions exceeded the strength of their commitment. Players must have the mental toughness to be not only indefatigable in match play but also to take on intimidating training and practice regimes.

**And I am NOT suggesting a twenty mile run as a test for would be soccer players!**

In soccer, tough minded backs are those who are always where an attacker doesn't want them to be. They are the players who can mark opponents touch tight, tackle incisively, intercept cleanly and who cannot be shaken off. They are the players who attack the ball. . . especially the fifty-fifty ball. . . with one hundred and one percent commitment. And if they lose out, rarely, the only sign they show is a hardening of the already mean glint in their eyes.

Tough minded players are the competitors to whom losing is unthinkable and who are prepared to train, practice and play until it becomes impossible.

### 2.2 Concentration.

Mental toughness, in a ninety minute action period, requires considerable powers of concentration, especially if a player is out of the action for substantial periods of time.

**Mentally, a tough minded player is never out of the action!**

Concentration isn't a gift, it's a skill; it can be learned and taught like any other skill. There are players who from very early ages show high degrees of mental toughness, the quality can be improved through practice: similarly with concentration. It is highly unlikely that players are born with these attributes. The implications for soccer players, teachers and coaches are obvious.

Practice may not make perfect but the right sort of practice of any kind of skill, psychological or physical, will bring about improvement.

## 2.3 Anticipation.

Outstanding backs 'read' opponents well and they read them all the time. They are always adjusting their positions, moving to cover other defenders, to intercept the ball, to 'close down' potentially dangerous opponents and generally to block opposing attackers. Good attackers work hard and patiently to achieve positions near to goal which place defenders in two minds. Good full-backs are rarely if ever caught in two minds because they take action decisions early and positively. By doing so they clarify the action options. . . and the minds. . . of co-defenders.

A full-back who is indecisive creates uncertainty among other defenders. In the last line of defense it is better to be decisive and wrong rather than indecisive and still wrong!

Indecision not only makes the full-back himself ineffective, it makes other defenders take actions about which they are unsure and to which their commitment will be less than total. That's the beginning of nervous, shaky defensive play. Full backs must learn to out-think opponents: in other words to anticipate their intentions. That means becoming very perceptive students of all players' mannerisms: their 'body language' in fact. To any perceptive observer, an opponent's body language will reveal how much attention he gives to 'addressing' the ball before passing it long or short: off one foot or the other: on the ground or through the air and so on. All players 'set' themselves, instinctively almost, long before they begin to take skillful action. 'Setting' involves getting their bodies or certain limbs ready so that when the right opportunity to apply skill occurs they can act immediately.

All players have different preferred angles at which they place the ball 'off' their standing feet to give them the best swing at it. These are their personal skill habits: they rarely change or lose them.

Players need to know if their opponents can stop an action and change instantly to another. They must study and remember how opponents' movement patterns, the action of their arms and their legs, change as they prepare for explosive action or to use certain skills. The clues are there if the full-back. . . or any other player. . . is prepared to study them.

## 2.4 Composure.

Full backs may be out of the action for long periods but suddenly the game can change. Long periods of inactivity may be interspersed with bursts of hectic action perhaps in or near to the penalty area.

Not only must a back be decisive he must be calm and confident. In these circumstances attackers have defending opponents under pressure. A mistake by an attacker may be written off as a 'good try' or 'bad luck'; a similar error by a back usually is critical; excuses are unacceptable.

A good defender remains unshakably calm even under severe pressure. In doing so, he can provide that element of surprise which is a basic principle of attack and defense. Bringing the ball under instant control, faking a clearance kick and then calmly passing or dribbling the ball out of the penalty area and out of danger often has a shattering effect on the confidence and enthusiasm of opponents.

**Whatever the circumstances, exceptional full-backs keep their 'cool'.**

## 2.5 Tackling skill.

The first four attributes, broadly speaking, are psychological. The next attribute is the skill of winning tackles for the ball.

German national coach, Berti Vogts, was one of the tightest man to man markers that I have ever seen. He never aspired to the technical and athletic elegance of Franz Beckenbauer but as a destroyer Vogts was supreme. Not only did he mark tightly, he tackled with razor sharpness and recovered with blinding speed. Beckenbauer and Vogts were a perfect match. Marco Tardelli, the play anywhere world class Italy and Juventus player, had the same qualities. Shirt tight marking and totally incisive tackling were his hallmark and the mental toughness to subdue anyone and everyone, almost.

These players mesmerize and contain opponents by jockeying them into traps from which escape is nearly impossible. The final 'coup' is the trap-tight tackle, escape impossible. Real full-backs must be able to tackle the ball away from opponents. The tackling skills. . . the front block tackle, the side block tackle, the sliding tackle from behind together with the associated skills of lifting the ball out of the tackle or pulling it away from an opponent are largely ignored by today's teachers and coaches.

Many coaches argue that tackling practice involves the risk of injury but any sort of realistic, which is to say effective, practice involves risk. In fact the risk of injury in match play is significantly reduced when players have been well taught and coached to tackle, and to resist tackles, skillfully.

The first requirement is to be determined to tackle! Too many defenders are determined not to tackle at any cost. The cost, usually, involves goals given away and I do mean 'given'. Massed, zonal, defensive systems have restricted playing space to such an extent that bad defenders have been encouraged to think that position and patience will cause opponents to give the ball away sooner or later. Bad players may do so, good players won't!

In England, 'doubling up' on opponents, diagram 1, whereby a first defending

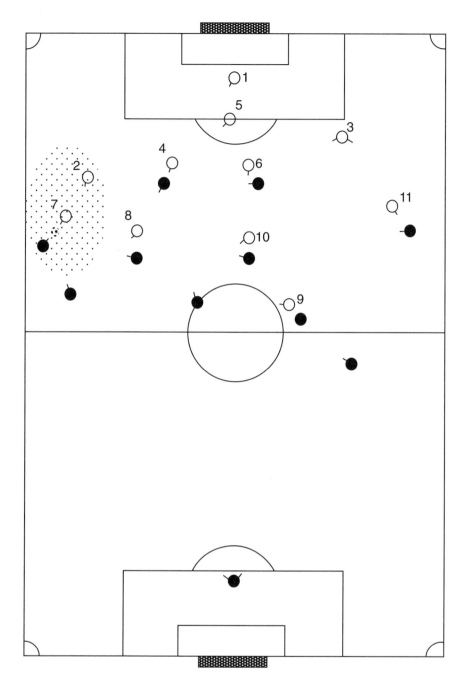

**Diagram 1**. 'Doubling up' in defense.

player is closely covered by a second has reduced the need for tackling skill, or so coaches think. They believe, wrongly, that they only need to hustle to stand a better than even chance of being given the ball.

Excessive numbers of players merely filling defensive spaces produces poor defenders. In English professional soccer, deploying a large number of players behind the ball often ensures that unskillful, careless attackers give the ball away without too much defensive pressure and certainly without the need to tackle. The game is poorer because of it.

Unsure defenders have become unwilling to put their feet into tackles decisively. Any full-back worth the name, one against one, must be able to contain an opponent, jockey him into a tight trap and tackle for the ball with certainty.

A particularly skillful or perhaps very quick attacker may warrant special tactical attention but this does not justify the massed deployment of defenders who cannot defend!

The sustained success of German international teams has been based upon the continuing availability of quick tackling, tight marking, tough-minded defenders. That is not to imply that the Germans' world number one spot has been achieved exclusively through defensive skills but they have certainly helped.

When a team hasn't got the ball, to get it requires determined marking and skillful tackling in all one against one situations.

In some ways, weaknesses in the wide back positions are more difficult to hide tactically than are weaknesses among central backs, for reasons which we shall analyze later.

## 2.6  Control.

The next attribute which is vital in a first class full-back is instant, close control. With this quality, backs, even under pressure, have a depressing effect on opponents and a confidence boosting effect on their team mates. Traditionally, full-backs were expected to lack the touch and control of say mid-field players. The more hectic the play the greater the likelihood of backs making controlling errors. Modern full-backs don't have these problems. Paul Breitner of Bayern München and West Germany during the seventies, golden years for German soccer, was probably the best all round full-back in the world. Breitner not only dominated opponents tactically and athletically, he had the technical qualities of a high class mid-field player, a position in which he often played when he moved from Germany to Spain.

In contemporary soccer, the value of technique cannot be exaggerated. Some backs show class, or if you prefer it 'style', when they break out from defense into open attacking play. But this obvious evidence of technical virtuosity sometimes hides serious defensive deficiencies. True technical qualities are best seen when players are involved in desperate defense.

**Outstanding full-backs never defend desperately! They don't need to.**

## 2.7  Speed Agility.

Soccer involves the need for two distinct kinds of agility.

First there is the capacity for changing position on the pitch in different, often unexpected directions at optimum speed while using or preparing to use the skills of the game.

Second there is the need for changing the position and the shape of one's body often, again, at optimum speed and while employing one or more of the game's skills.

The latter type of agility is most commonly seen in the play of a goalkeeper but not exclusively so.

The first type of speed agility is of particular importance to full-backs.

Attackers often employ elaborate and very quickly executed interchanges of position to confuse and to draw defenders out of position. Backs must track or cover these moves, 'just in case', and then return to the areas for which they are singularly responsible as part of the team's integrated defensive system. These movements have to be carried out very quickly not least because they are reactive.

Usually a back can only move when his opponent has already begun to move which means that the defender must move that much quicker.

These bursts of activity may be required frequently when a defense is under pressure. The back may be required to move little more than five to ten yards. Over such short distances it is not possible for a player to develop a true sprinting stride in the athletic sense. He may have to make these 'agility runs' in a semi crouched position in which his leg and thigh muscles are not able to relax and in which therefore fatigue develops. . . unless, that is, his agility speed training has enabled him to cope. In recent years the athletic. . . and the gymnastic. . . demands of soccer have increased significantly. Training methods have shifted away from quantity to quality. Long distance, even paced, training runs have been replaced by high quality agility or athletic speed training. . . or they should have!

Intelligent, well-trained, forward-looking coaches in the top soccer countries are devising technical practices which can be adapted to meet either agility speed requirements or technical needs. Examples of these activities are shown later in this book.

Those then are the attributes required by a top class full-back and they lead us logically into an examination of the full-backs' responsibilities in play.

# Chapter 3
# **Responsibilities**

Τ he most important requirement of all for high class full-backs is that they should understand their responsibilities and have their functional priorities absolutely clear in their minds.

### 3.1 Ultimate Defense.
Backs provide the final defensive curtain in front of the goalkeeper; they and he must control the space between them so that penetration by an opponent with the ball, or to receive it, is minimized and if achieved rendered instantly ineffective. Stating the obvious? Maybe, but understanding that requirement and others like it is the basis for a crystal clear appreciation of what the full-back must be about.

This requires the full-back to be highly capable in the following skills.

### 3.11 Marking and Shot Blocking.
Any movement of opponents towards or into the space referred to must be resisted. Either the space must be filled before the opponents make their moves or the opponents must be marked tightly as they move into that space. Marking an opponent tightly means that the back must be so close to his opponent that the opponent cannot shoot or turn to shoot. If achieving that objective means that the attacker has to be allowed or encouraged to select another less dangerous option then that must be the order of priority.

Preventing shots has the highest priority for all defenders. If attackers can't shoot they can't score.

In the highest priority areas, diagram 2, when an instant decision is required, a back must mark rather than cover another defender. That priority must be observed even by the sweeper, the free back. While every attempt is made to keep the libero free of marking and challenging duties, if a shot is 'on', he like any other back, must stop or block it.

### 3.12 Pass Blocking.
If the ball cannot be delivered into high priority shooting areas, diagram 2, effective shots cannot be made. The shaded areas are those from which the most dangerous passes leading to effective shots are most likely to come. Attackers must be prevented from delivering those passes.

All full-backs must deter or physically block any attempt to pass the ball into the penalty area.

**Real full-backs will, 'pretenders' won't!**

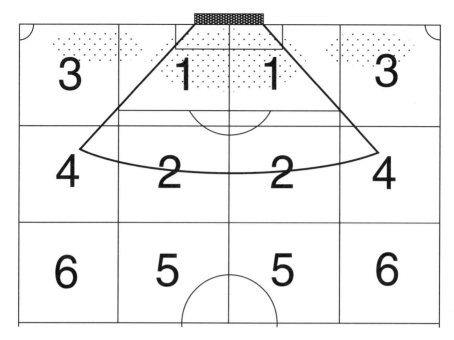

**Diagram 2.** Key scoring and delivery areas and therefore defensive priority areas.

Experienced backs learn to judge the exact moment when an opponent will try to get in his cross-field pass. No more than inches from the ball and as it is kicked, the back 'presents' his foot to block it. It's not as dangerous as it sounds if the back is prepared to watch and wait. If he lunges for the ball, it's a certainty that he will miss it and probably be kicked into the bargain as the attacker's kicking foot follows through.

### 3.13 Containing.

A full-back may encourage an attacker to keep the ball or to pass it to another attacker, so long as the pass is 'outside' the defense and to an attacker who, himself, will be under close control instantly, diagram 3.

Offering an opponent a controllable action option is preferable to risking and missing a tackle thereby allowing him make an effective pass or shot.

Controlling the space to limit an attacker's action options is an important defensive skill. Limiting his options while persuading him to select one particular option is very high class defending indeed.

### 3.14 Covering.

When a back is sure that he has no immediate marking responsibility, he must cover someone who has.

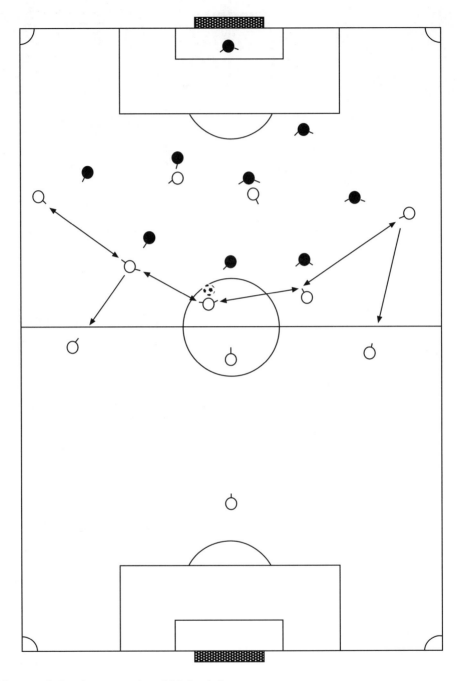

**Diagram 3.** Passing moves 'outside' the defense.

In zonal defense, where the action is close to his zone of responsibility, a back must provide close cover behind any other defender who is confronting an opponent with the ball. Diagram 1.

Effective cover is achieved when a defender can instantly challenge any attacker who dribbles past another defender preferably before that attacker regains control over the ball. A covering defender can also control the flow of opponents' play by altering his angle of cover. Diagram 4. The distance at which the player takes up cover is crucially important. Too far from the forward defender and he cannot get at the attacker soon enough. Too near and a quick moving attacker may beat him and the first defender in the same movement.

## 3.15 Balancing Defense.

In all defensive systems, backs either pivot around the central defenders, diagram 5 (a), or slide across the field to consolidate central defense, diagram 5 (b).

The further he is from the ball, the greater the back's responsibility for balancing the defense by moving into more central positions. Doing so, he reduces possibilities for opponents to pass or move 'inside' the defensive structure. The exception is when a wide back has to mark a dangerous opponent very tightly, one to one. His opponent may move into the most unlikely positions to draw him away from an integrated defensive relationship with other players. Where this happens, a picket player in front of the backs, diagram 6 (a) or a sweeper behind may be deployed to watch for lack of cover or balance and, if necessary, to provide it. diagram 6 (b).

The 'sweeper' system has encouraged some full-backs to think that the sweeper's primary covering function relieves them of any responsibility for cover or balance. They are dangerously mistaken.

Space made available behind or within a defense at the right time is always a potential source of danger.

## 3.16 Communicating.

Backs positioned furthest from immediate action have an important responsibility for informing team mates more immediately involved what is going on behind them. And for our purposes goalkeepers are also backs.

Defenders need not be over worried about what they can see; they have to be extremely concerned about opponents who sneak into threatening space behind them.

Gifted attackers, especially goalscorers, can 'disappear' from play and reappear in the most unlikely areas, usually unmarked and unnoticed. The 'far side backs and other defenders away from immediate play must be the eyes in the backs of other defenders' heads. Intelligent, tactically aware full-backs are worth their weight in precious metal; they see trouble coming before it becomes serious. This sense of danger enables them to control the actions of other defenders. All players 'ball watch' some of the time: they must, occasionally. But defenders who are hypnotized by the ball are dangerous. . . to their own teams. Their attention is easily drawn away from

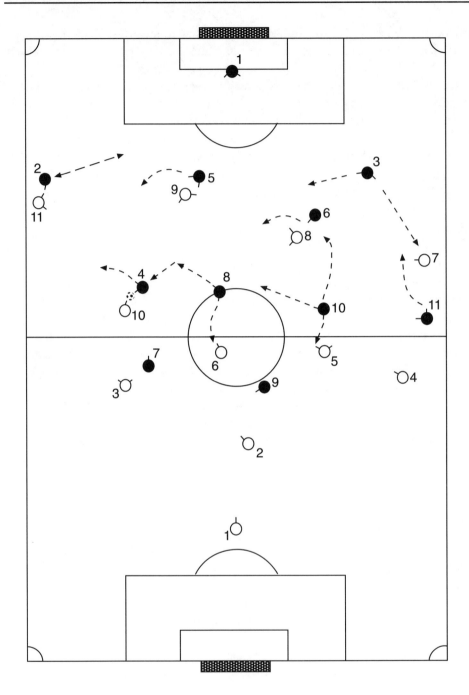

**Diagram 4.** Altering the covering angle.

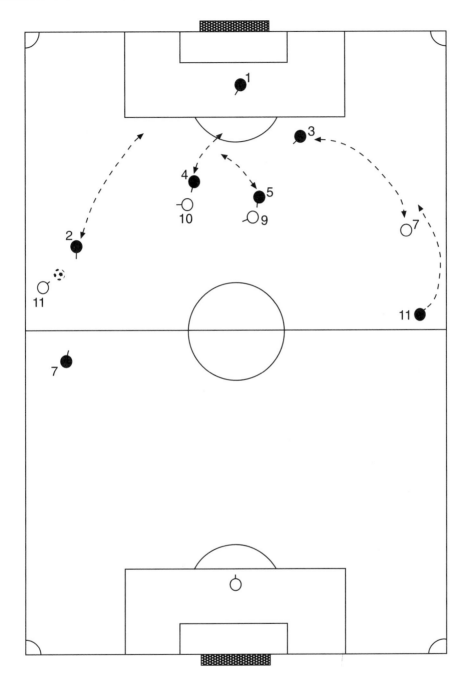

**Diagram 5 (a)**. Pivoting Backs.

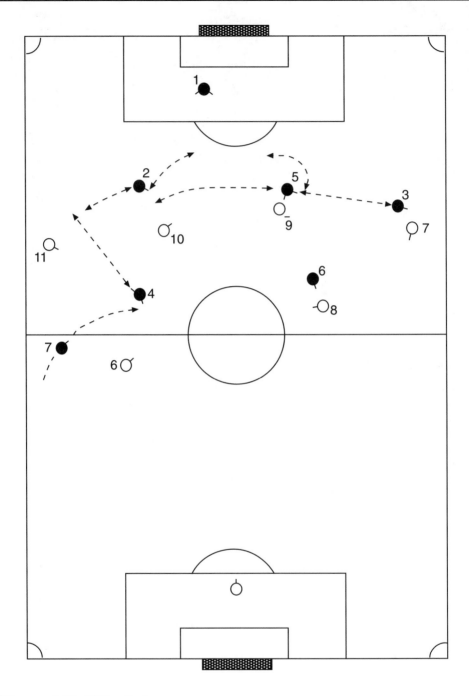

**Diagram 5 (b).** Sliding Backs.

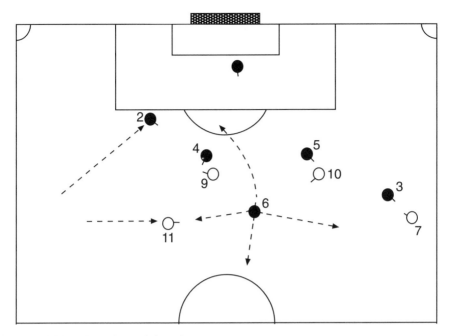

**Diagram 6 (a).** Black 6 the picket player.

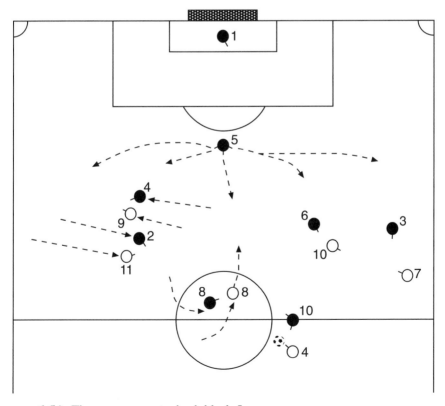

**Diagram 6 (b):** The sweeper center back black 5.

the opportunists, players always looking to steal into striking positions unnoticed.

**It is the responsibility of a 'far side' back to notice everything!**

And before we go any further, 'far side' refers to the area beyond the goal viewed from a player positioned on the other side of the field.

Good communication between players is the basis for fully integrated team play, in attack and in defense. It is based upon mutual trust and on clear understanding. Much like authors and their readers come to think of it. Players must learn. . . and therefore they must be taught. . . how to inform other players of the best moves to make so that inter-play becomes second nature. . . or seems to.

## 3.17  Countering.

Soccer played well is attacking soccer, soccer played to score goals. Soccer played badly is negative soccer, soccer played to avoid losing by thinking defensively even when in position to attack.

The backs and the goalkeeper are likely to find themselves in possession of the ball at the time of a 'turn-over' more than other players. They must have the perception to see, instantly, possibilities for counter-attack. To launch a counter attack from a position deep in a team's defensive quarter of the field with opponents in strength around the ball, may be to invite trouble: nothing ventured nothing gained. In the same position, opponents may be heavily committed as far from their own goal as they are ever likely to be. Desperate counter-attack may be justified only when a team is losing with two or three minutes to play say. Clearly thought out counter attack is always worth the effort.

Having been severely pressured, the immediate need of a team regaining possession of the ball is to control it securely. The nearer to goal the situation is, the more it may pay the attacking team to exert pressure to regain it. That may be the best time for defenders to counter attack.

In modern soccer, the onus is on the backs for ensuring that the ball is secure while a team reorganizes for attack. Backs are rarely put under the pressure to which other players, especially mid-field players, are subjected. Maybe they should be. As I have said, soccer has not yet adopted the total 'pressing' game; it will.

Fast 'break outs' into attack are likely to produce, briefly, three against three or four against four situations. Occasionally the countering side may even outnumber defenders. Backs must secure ball possession to establish effective, surprise attacking platforms.

To exploit these situations at speed, backs need to have vision. They need to assess possible attacking options even when their opponents have the ball. Exploiting opportunities, and they may be rare, demands very quick execution of precise skills but above all the perception to see these opportunities when they are likely to occur. It is one thing for a back to see the chance to dribble the ball decisively past one or two opponents and make a significant attacking break out, it is quite another if he lacks the tight, individual ball control and the agility to enable him to do so confidently.

The implication for coaches concerned with the very early development of young players is that they must be given experience in all positions whatever their final choice of playing position may be.

In the 'advanced' soccer countries too much emphasis is placed on putting players into positional strait jackets too soon. Early experience of high class competition may seem to be a good thing but experience is a two edged tool; it may show us what is possible but it also teaches us what isn't. . . painfully at times.

All skills are best learned when and where it doesn't matter too much if they fail, in practice. If players are always playing in games of importance, in which results matter, they cannot afford to try new skills. They learn to use limited, safe skills, skills which, more often than not, are defensive or negative.

## 3.18 Consolidating.

In the German World Cup winning team of 1990, the left back, Brehme, was probably one of the three best full-backs in the world at the time. He had considerable speed, a steely determination to give an opponent nothing. . . other than a hard time. . . , quickness in the tackle and a very responsible attitude towards the rest of his defenders. When the going got tough Mr. Brehme definitely got going!

In addition to his defensive attributes, Brehme could and would surge forward on attacking runs, giving and receiving passes deep in the opponents' half of the field. Near to opponents' penalty areas he possessed a deadly shot with either foot. Frequently he outflanked opposing backs and delivered crosses with variation and accuracy. He was truly a wing back. Modern full-backs must be capable of exploiting all attacking possibilities by accepting opportunities to dribble, pass and shoot, certainly they must be able to score.

In practice, the backs should be given opportunities to develop the two and three player interpassing moves necessary for players to penetrate packed, opposing defenses. Crossing the ball at different angles and with varying speeds is a specialized kicking skill; the wide backs need specialized practice in acquiring it.

In the highly successful Liverpool team in England a few years ago, all players were expected to shoot accurately however infrequent the opportunities available. They developed and improved their skill by regular tactical and technical shooting practice. There is no other way.

# Chapter 4
# Tactics in Principle and Practice

**M**odern soccer strategies are often devised to minimize the chances of losing. Winning is achieved by punishing such errors as opponents choose to make. What happens when they don't make too many is a good question rarely answered. Commitment to sustained attack is seen usually as a last throw of the dice.

In European professional soccer, huge monetary incentives have induced degrees of strategical fear approaching inertia almost. Add instant exposure to television analysis of the most critical kind and you have a recipe for disaster.

Even so, I take an optimistic view of the future merely because there is nowhere else to go defensively. Fortune will favor the brave: those teams prepared to match defenders, player for player, with forwards. The softest of all defensive options, the pass back to the goalkeeper must be totally eliminated and goalkeepers must be confined to their penalty areas.

Punish ALL deliberate fouls with penalty kicks and we could have ourselves a great game again.

Even so, soccer will continue to demand that,

(a) forward moving players are marked tightly,

(b) key attacking spaces are controlled by defenders and

(c) cover is provided against the possibility of attacking breakthroughs in key areas.

Most goals are scored from central positions well inside the penalty area: less frequently from its edge. It follows that central defense and the positional relationships between central backs are vitally important factors in team success.

### 4.1 Depth and Balance in Defense.

Two of the basic principles of defensive play are depth and balance. Depth is established between three or more defending players when their positional relationship is triangular or multi triangular.

The relationship in play between, say, a right back, a wide mid-field player and the central mid-field player inside him is based upon distances.

a) The distance between the foremost defender and the opponent with the ball or an opponent in need of tight marking.

b) The distance between the front defender and the other two which will enable either to contain an opponent with the ball should he defeat the first defender.

c) The distances between each of the three triangulated players which make any attempts by opponents to pass the ball through the triangle or over it highly improbable.

The basis of effective defensive triangulation is the covering relationship between any two of the players making up the triangle.

In diagram 7, the distance between the right back and the central mid-field player has become too great. The two attackers will have a much better chance of interpassing, or dribbling and interpassing, to beat the two defenders, black 7 and 8. If the deep player, white 6, can move very quickly and as late as possible to support the attack, there is the chance of the attack outnumbering the defenders, however briefly, 3 to 2.

In diagram 8, three central backs have set up a sound defensive triangle with one player, black 5, acting as a free central back or 'sweeper'. His role is easy while the two central attackers, white 9 and 10, remain in close support of each other. If they stretch their positional relationship, two of the three central defenders must stretch their own especially if they mark the attackers man for man. Diagram 9.

Depth and cover will be difficult to maintain. Without the free back or libero there will not be any. Two of the three defenders must now decide whether they should mark and follow the two central attackers or whether they should maintain the solid triangular relationship while tracking (following at a distance) the attackers' movements.

This is the issue central to any dilemma in which coaches find themselves when they search for black or white answers to the man marking or space marking (zonal) conundrum. It is difficult to be categorical, talented attackers will set problems for both systems. That's how and why they are talented.

Rigid tactics usually are the products of rigid minds; both produce inflexible players, players without initiative or imagination.

Nevertheless, defenders, especially backs, who cannot mark opponents out of the game when required, present serious defensive deficiencies.

Tight man for man marking is the fundamental basis of all sound defensive organization, even for zonal defense. Think that one through!

## 4.11 Twin Centre-Back Play.
Where team organization allows two central backs to choose when each will  cover or mark, the following tactical adaptations may be employed.

### (a) Tight and Loose.
One specific centre back becomes the striker's marker. The striker is likely to have certain special attributes and it is logical that his marker should have the qualities to

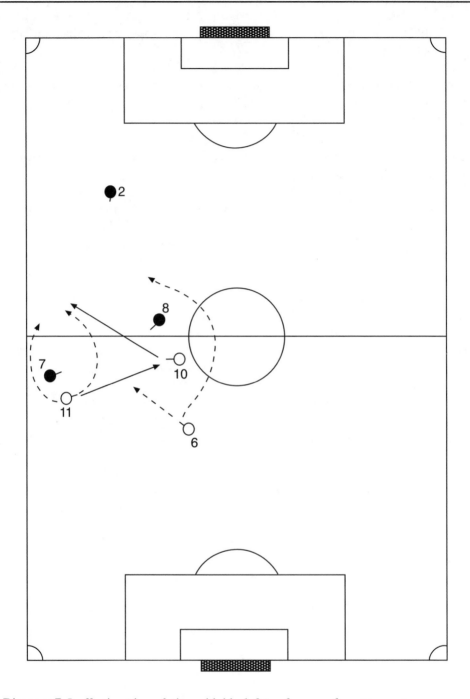

**Diagram 7**. Ineffective triangulation with black 2 too far away from teammates.

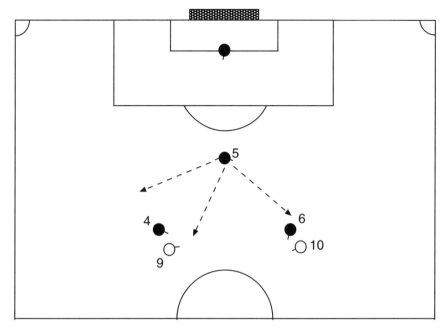

**Diagram 8.** Triangulation with the sweeper and tight marking backs.

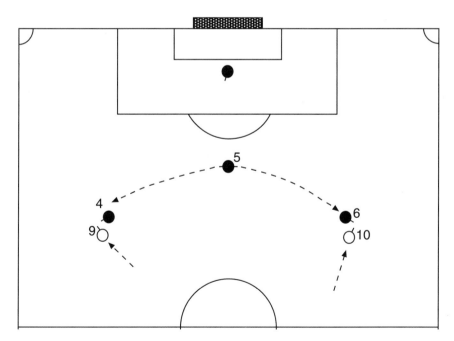

**Diagram 9.** Stretching a defensive triangle.

counter those attributes. The second centre back becomes in effect a free back responsible for all central cover. The true sweeper has more detailed integration responsibilities with all the backs and some mid-field players as well.

### (b) Pass Over Play.

Alternatively each centre back may 'pick up' the striker as and when he moves into that back's area of the pitch. They transfer (pass over) marking responsibility as the striker moves out of and into relevant areas close to each centre back. A right footed centre back will operate more comfortably on the right side of the defensive area and vice versa. He will find a right footed central attacker easier to deal with if he learns to 'jockey' (maneuver) the attacker onto that player's left foot!

Attackers with the ball must never be allowed free choice of direction or of the preferred foot. Force right footed players to move to their left and at best they can be severely embarrassed; at worst their play becomes more predictable. Occasionally team tactical considerations may require rules to be reversed. A team's defensive game plan may be to force all opposing attacks in-field and away from the wings. A centre back will jockey opponents towards central areas, Doing so, he will be more comfortable if his 'inside' foot is the stronger.

Where a team deploys one central back to mark and the other to cover, the rest of the defensive structure can be part zonal, part man-to-man. The covering back allows that latitude. In 'pass over' play where each centre back collects the striker if or when he moves towards him, the rest of the defense must be zonal. One attacker moving relatively freely is permissible: another attacker with similar freedom would pose impossible defensive problems.

Mixed defense, zonal and man-to-man, is a possibility only when markers are absolved from any other marking or covering responsibilities. The rest of the defense can then accept zones of responsibility and ignore the movements of the markers and their opponents, even within the full defense. Man-to-man marking is intended to obliterate certain specific opponents leaving the rest of the defense to get on with the game.

Where attackers are allowed to move relatively freely in certain areas, it is the responsibility of the nearest defenders to track them or mark them tightly as circumstances demand.

Effective communication and instant response based upon mutual respect between the backs are absolutely vital.

Moving from a tracking position to a close marking commitment sounds easy enough but it demands extreme vigilance and concentration. Defenders fall into bad habits from time to time. Where both centre backs are reluctant to move into close marking positions quickly, a sweeper behind them or a picket in front are absolutely vital. Someone must pick up one of the attackers quickly. Lazy defenders convince themselves that they will be able to get by on opponents' mistakes and their own interceptions. They may do so, for a time, against poor attackers. When they fail, as they will against clever attackers, the result will be devastating.

Strangely, where centre backs, especially veteran centre backs, have developed bad marking habits, they are often unreasonably resistant to corrective coaching and practice.

## (c) Two on Two.

Where two centre backs are deployed against two central attackers, cover is possible only when each in turn partially 'drops off' the attacker for whom he is responsible, leaving the other centre back to mark one attacker as tightly as circumstances dictate.

The two defenders will press up tightly against each of the two opponents until they judge that a dangerous forward pass is 'on'. The pass may seem to be towards an attacker's feet or into the space behind or to the side of the centre backs. One centre back will tell his team mate to remain marking tightly while he drops back and 'off' his own opponent to give cover. The ball cannot be played effectively behind the deep defender and if it is played over and behind the marking defender the covering centre back should intercept it. He hopes!

If, in these circumstances, a pass is played to the feet of the 'far-side' central attacker, white 10 in diagram 10, there will be two defensive possibilities. The covering central defender, black 5, can move quickly to shorten (close down) the distance between himself and the pass receiver He has the time it takes for the ball to travel there plus whatever anticipation time he can conjure up. Alternatively his team mate, black 6, 'drops off' his marking position to give his team mate the necessary cover.

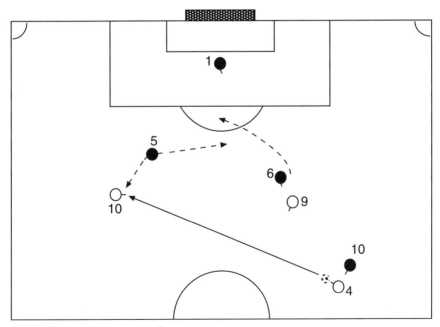

**Diagram 10.** Balancing central defense.

The alternative is for the two central defenders to agree that, wherever possible, one of them will always move into the marking position while the other always provides cover, diagram 11. One central defender is good at marking and enjoys it while the other doesn't mark well but covers effectively and enjoys a controlling function. A problem for both occurs when two central attackers have superior speed and take up positions well away from each other, thereby disturbing the defenders' distance relationship.

The problem now is one of distance and time i.e. speed. How far apart can the central backs be drawn before a player who should be covering hasn't got the time to move into a covering position? Clearly the quicker the two defenders are and the greater their powers of anticipation, the greater the distance which they can allow to develop between them. This problem indicates, for those who want to see, the need for a sweeper behind two markers or a picket player who can 'pick up' any attacker whose positional play makes the 'travel relationship' between the two centre backs difficult to sustain. The picket player will always threaten the line of any pass aimed for either of the two central attackers and even if such passes arrive, so will he.

Where and when the two central backs are half way to changing from covering to marking and vice versa, they are 'square' at which time final defense is very vulnerable. That's the price to be paid for playing without a free centre back.

Setting and solving problems may be the single most important attribute in a soccer coach not only during match play, where he may directly influence the result, but especially during practice.

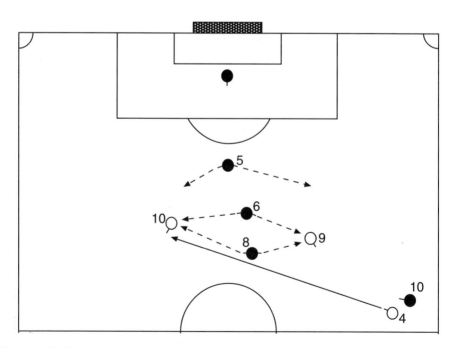

**Diagram 11.** One marker tight and one loose: the value of a picket player black 8.

Effective coaching at the highest levels of performance depends on a coach's ability to design practice situations which set realistic problems out of which coaches and players can come up with profitable answers. And drills are for robots not thinkers.

## 4.12  Flat Back Four.

Most central defenders in England are deployed in pairs,  2 v 1 or 2 v 2. As the threat of attacking penetration becomes imminent, both central backs may push up very tightly against their opponents inviting the ball to be passed over their heads. Pushing up in this way threatens to catch strikers in off-side positions. If the ball is played forward, one of the central defenders drops off late and quickly in that expectation. His judgment and timing have to be inch perfect to cope with the modern off side law. When players were allowed to pass back freely to goalkeepers this was a fail-safe option. Without that choice the flat backs have no easy escape outlet should the timing of the off-side trap be poor.

A problem also emerges when opponents work the ball into a wide position and a pass is angled across the field and behind the far-side centre back. Mid-field or even opposing wide backs running from deep positions are difficult to pick up and mark, diagram 12.

A cross field pass eliminates interference from the 'keeper and central defenders are drawn even further away from each other. Similarly if the passing player can deliver the ball up-field and behind the central defender with 'fade', a striker has a better chance of winning the race for possession and again the central backs are being isolated from each other .

It is crucially important for the wide backs to get their defending priorities right. They must forego tight marking responsibilities against wide attackers and balance the defense by covering behind the threatened centre back.

When play is clearly developing down one defensive flank, the 'far-side' full-back must balance the defense by moving towards centre field and into a covering position on the area central to goal and behind the two centre backs, diagram 13. This may require the far side defending winger to drop back and threaten to or actually mark his immediate opponent.

## 4.13  Balancing a Defense.

Balancing is a fundamental principle of collective defense. It enables the backs to resist penetration, from passes or players, into the spaces behind them or between the backs and the defenders in front of them. Attackers are compelled to pass and play around the outside of the defensive structure and the minimum of re-positioning allows the defense to consolidate against any change of attacking thrust.

In diagram 13, the black team is facing a break through down its left defensive flank. It is not certain that the attack will continue in that direction but it might. However it would require no great skill for the attacking thrust to be switched against central defense or even to the opposite (right) defensive flank. The defending team

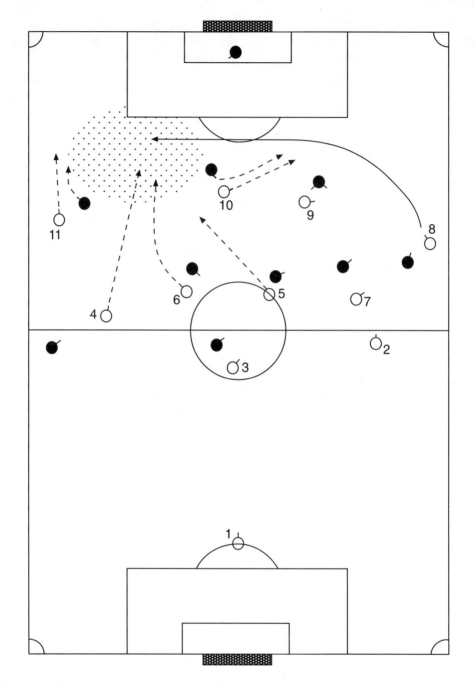

**Diagram 12.** Exposure of space behind a 'far-side' center back by attackers running from deep positions.

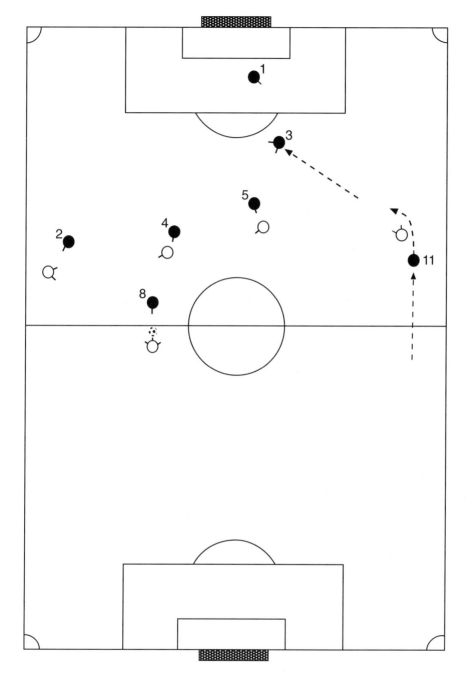

**Diagram 13.** The 'far side' back balancing in a full court position.

must remain balanced against all eventualities.

As attacking play is developed across the defensive front, the full-back opposite to the direction of thrust (far side), in this case black 3, must move to reduce the space between him and the goalkeeper and also behind the central defenders.

In the event of the opponents changing the threat from one flank to the other frequently, balance will be effected by both wide backs withdrawing into semi-covering positions, diagram 14. The attack may develop towards the unmarked wing attackers but it will still be outside the whole defense. If one of the wide attackers becomes the focus of attacking interplay, the full-back on the far side of the defense can adopt a full covering position.

## 4.14 The Sweeper Centre Back.

Twenty or thirty years ago, when an orthodox back alignment consisted of three backs, the wide backs needed to run considerable distances as they moved onto or dropped off their wing opponents to provide cover centrally. Opponents hid the intended direction of attacking thrust until the backs, pivoting around the central back to give him cover, were caught half way 'on' and half way 'off' their opponents. . . in other words in 'square' positions. Diagram 15. In this situation one shrewd pass between and behind the backs defeated all three.

Where the distances between two or more pivoting players are long, in the previous example perhaps as much as thirty yards, the time when the defenders are in poor covering positions is increased. Even in the twin centre back deployment, where the distance between the two players may be as little as ten yards, moving from a covering to a marking position leaves the central defense, as we have seen, too square for too long.

The deployment of a Sweeper (Libero) behind the other backs, with covering responsibilities behind as much of the back defensive line as possible, rendered laborious pivoting unnecessary. . . almost.

Where the sweeper is drawn into a supporting position towards the opposing ball holder, the far side back still has the responsibility for controlling defenders in front of him and thereby balancing his defense against a switch of attacking play.

Where an attack is developing against the left defensive flank, say, the libero (sweeper) will move over, or prepare to move over, to give cover and to resist if necessary any threat of penetration down that flank. By doing so he exposes space behind him at an angle to the goal which could be exploited by a clever attacker running on the blind-side of the far-side full-back. That full-back must balance his defense by cutting down the distance between the sweeper and central attacking areas. . . the high priority striking areas. In other words by pivoting on the central defense. Diagram 16.

Some coaches, particularly those who favor the negative use of off-side tactics, ask the far-side back to 'tuck in' towards the central defensive area rather than pivot behind it. From this position, in which the far side back has moved towards the danger area, he can gain a start in any race for passes played towards the central area,

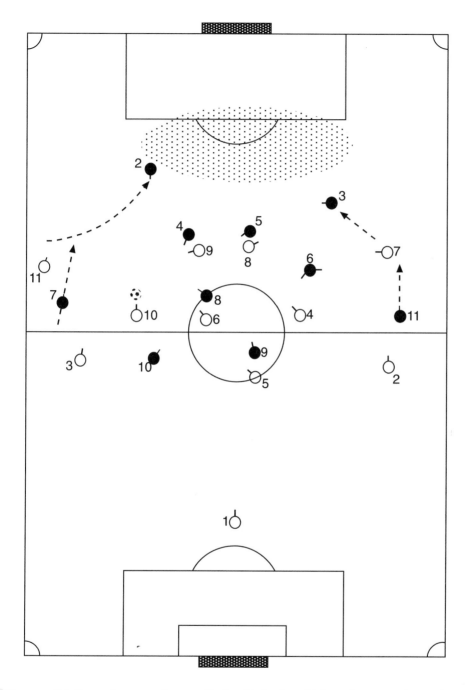

**Diagram 14.** Protecting central space: Both wide backs withdraw into central covering positions.

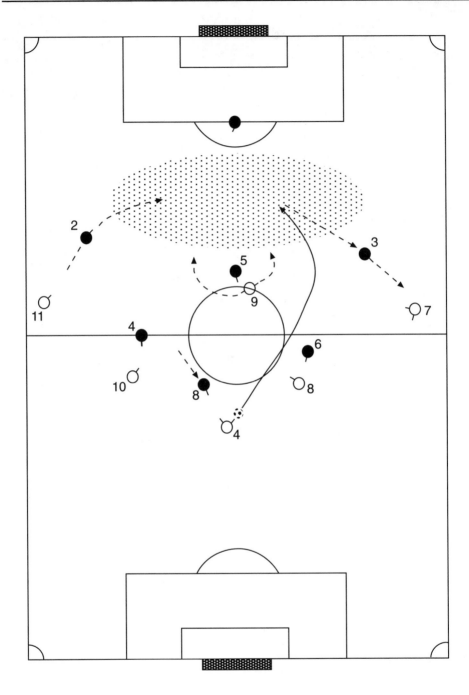

**Diagram 15.** Wide backs 'pivoting' and caught in square positions.

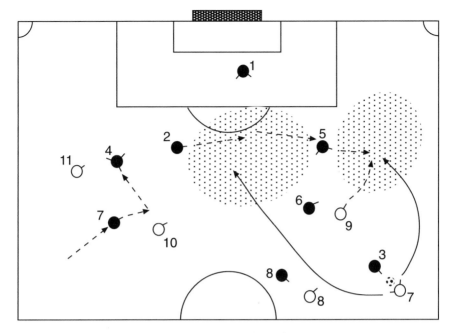

**Diagram 16.** Covering the sweeper and balancing the defense.

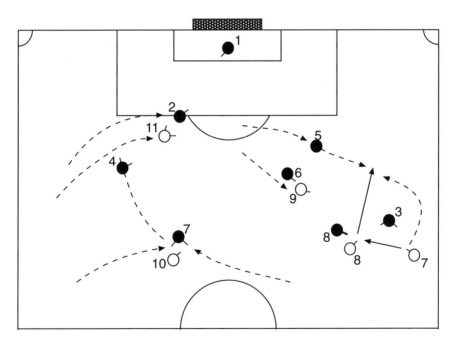

**Diagram 17.** Threatening the cover player, black 2 by joining him, white 11.

provided that an opponent doesn't move in field with him. Diagram 17. Additionally he is well positioned to move forward in concert with the other backs should the defensive 'controller' call for an off-side move.

'Tucking in' is risky because a long pass angled across field leaves the far-side back himself more exposed than he would be if he had pivoted and wherever they are, two defenders or ten, in line across the field are square and thereby vulnerable to through passes.

Any attacker able to judge passing angles and target areas well is likely to prove very difficult to handle. And of course very skillful passers over long distances enjoy these challenges to their skill.

Ruud Gullit, the Dreadlocked Dutchman, an excellent long passer relished any opportunity to test his skill against a flat back line. Holland's equally talented striker, Marco Van Basten, was more than likely to punish the slightest error of judgment by backs in these situations.

Off-side tactics are a legitimate part of the game although, in my belief, negative and hardly worth the risk.

The precondition to a Sweeper operating successfully is the ability of markers in front of him to mark tightly and to prevent opponents from turning towards goal with the ball. The markers must submit themselves to the Sweeper's ultimate control and direction. They do the donkey work which enables the Sweeper to look the elegant player that he should be but that's what tactics are about. . . using different skills and capacities in the best interests of team play.

According to the Sweeper's assessment of his own speed against the speed of opposing passers and pass receivers, he will move earlier and nearer or remain further away from what he estimates the target to be. If he 'shows himself' early in a possible intercepting position, almost certainly he will cause the passer to change his mind about the pass. He may have chosen this action because he is unhappy about defensive security in another area of the back line of defense.

In diagram 18, a first line defender, black 10, has been caught out of position momentarily, leaving a hole in the defense's primary defensive curtain (shaded area). By 'showing himself' deliberately early in a challenging position, the Sweeper is buying 'time' for the recovering defender to get into position. On the other hand, where the defense is well organized and the Sweeper is confident in the balancing ability of other back defenders, he may hold a position from which, to the passer, he looks unlikely to be able to interfere with the passing move. A perceptive Sweeper with speed. . . Germany's all-time great, Franz Beckenbauer, for example, . . . will wait for the passer to drop his eyes to concentrate on a good kicking contact, before accelerating smoothly to pick off the pass.

Great players hide their intentions and delay their movements until they are certain that their intended actions cannot be anticipated by opponents.

Cunning players, in all passing sports, move when an opponent's attention is concentrated elsewhere.

A word of caution; there are gifted ball passers who don't need to look at the ball when kicking it! Their wide angle (peripheral) vision seems to allow them to change

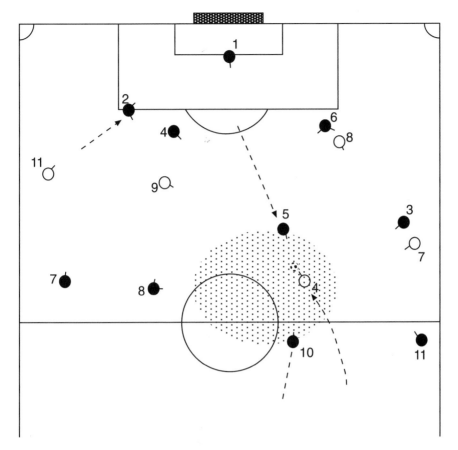

**Diagram 18.** The sweeper moves forward to plug a defensive hole temporarily.

their techniques very late indeed. For backs these are the real problem players but that's what makes the game of soccer the greatest game in the world; nothing in it can ever be a 24 carat certainty.

Great Sweepers. . . Liberos. . . . are best selected from outstanding mid-field play readers and play makers who don't enjoy perhaps the mid-field challenge and confrontation which modern soccer involves. Nature's sweepers are intellectual players, players who see the game like chess in which moves and counter moves must be planned and created patiently. They may or may not have special physical attributes. . . size, height, speed, power and so on. Sweepers come in all shapes and sizes but the good ones read the game like you and I read a good book, this one for example!

Industrious soccer is not a capacity to be sought in potential Sweepers. They are calm, considerate players, in total command of themselves and of any situation in which they are involved. Excitable, aggressive or explosive personalities are contradictory to everything that a Sweeper stands for.

Earlier, I set out the priorities for defenders, first among which was the need to prevent shots on goal. A Sweeper stays out of the action unless he is guaranteed possession of the ball. Occasionally opposing attackers will open the defensive curtains in front of him, diagram 18.

Central attackers may draw their markers to the sides opening up the possibility for a central thrust by quick and late moving mid-field players. In these circumstances the sweeper must join the action decisively to move forward to contain the attacker, out of scoring range if possible, or to block his shot.

When any back is drawn forward towards the ball out of a covering or even out of a marking commitment, near to goal, the challenge must be committed and positive. The Sweeper, or any other defending player, must be willing to put any part of his body in the way of the shot. The nearer he is to his opponent when he does so the more successful he is likely to be, even if it hurts.

Backs expect heroism from goalkeepers when they are required to make diving challenges at attackers' feet, even at the risk of painful contact. Goalkeepers have the right to expect similar commitments from out-field defenders.

## 4.15 Sliding Backs.

When committed forward, the Sweeper is drawn into a 'no win' situation. To minimize the danger, other backs slide across field to pick up attackers as and when necessary.

The basic principle is that the more central the attacker the higher his marking priority. The wider the attacker, the lower his marking priority. This means that any defender must be prepared to leave a wide opponent unmarked in order to pick up a free attacker in a more central position. The wide player may seem dangerously positioned but less so than the more central player. These sliding moves by defenders from one opponent to another must be done instantly and without question.

In diagram 19, one of the central markers, black 4, realizing that the Sweeper will be exposed by white 9's attacking thrust, leaves his opponent, white 10, to contain or deflect the opponent's drive for goal. As he does so the full-back behind him, black 2, leaves his opponent and slides over to pick up white 10, the attacker left unmarked. Attackers may still expose the defense but it will be in a slightly less dangerous position and the defense as a whole will have gained valuable seconds to re-group.

Sliding defense has to be timed to perfection and depends totally on mutual confidence between defenders. Come to think of it, all successful defensive organization does.

If the containing move towards the player with the ball is made without warning, the defender expected to slide across to pick up another opponent may be slow to react and the defense will remain vulnerable. The solution is in communication. The backs must talk to each other in understandable language early enough for the need for certain actions to be seen and understood. A defensive controller is vital and no one is better placed for this role than the defender furthest from the action: more often than not the sweeper.

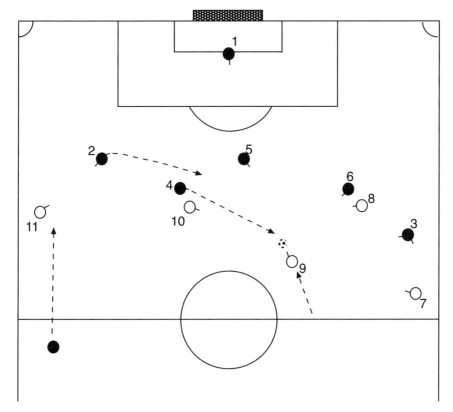

**Diagram 19**. A sliding screen to protect the sweeper: black 5.

The Sweeper's role in modern soccer has been greatly expanded to use his often superior skills and the space available to him in building up and even occasionally concluding attacking play. The German World Cup team in Argentina, in 1978, varied their attacking base at the back by allowing any two from three central defensive players to initiate and support attacking moves. And in defensive circumstances any one of the three would act as the Sweeper.

Back defenders, with the appropriate skills and athletic attributes, can pose difficult problems when they choose to counter attack from deep defensive positions. If soccer success is to be built upon high levels of all-round skill in a large number of players, as surely it is, a team made up of good liberos might do very well indeed.

In reality of course successful teams have a fine balance of different temperaments and different personalities. A team of Sweepers might be fascinating to watch, their game intricate and elegant but they might lack the cutting edge and the steely resolve which goal scoring and goal stopping in their different ways require.

## 4.16 Twin Sweepers.

In the 1974 World Cup finals in West Germany, the Argentinian team used two free backs in certain matches and strangely enough few opposing teams caught on to the problem or to its solution.

The Argentine team was deployed as in diagram 20. Often, during the second periods and playing to win without losing. . . if you know what I mean. . . Argentina deliberately split the team into two distinct 'halves'. Six outfield players stayed back all the time and four became out and out strikers: no midfield. Counter attack was based upon very fast throw-outs from the goalkeeper whenever he could deliver them beyond the opposing mid-field players. If he couldn't they kept the ball. Argentina played without a mid-field as such. Meanwhile the twin sweepers rendered angled cross-field passes, the passes most used to defeat the single sweeper, so much wasted effort.

Although not significantly successful in 1974, probably because they were preparing for 1978 in their own country, it was an interesting example of tactical innovation. Unique player deployments set difficult and unusual problems for their opponents.

During World Cup '66, in England, I thought that Argentina had probably the best all round team in the competition. Their centre backs, Perfumo and Albrecht were the quickest players I have seen when moving to contain, cover, intercept or to tackle against central attackers; and when they tackled they meant it!

Other than where used to develop a positive attacking platform, two free central backs is a luxury few teams could afford. Any team indulging in such extravagance must find itself outnumbered by the same number of 'free' players in other parts of the field.

Any team using permanent numerical superiority in one part of the field must pay for it in another. It's amazing how long some teams get away with it though!

## 4.17 The Picket Player or Front Sweeper.

(Picket: a person positioned outside property, often by industrial strike action, to prevent the unwanted from entering)

A picket player patrols the area in front of central backs to prevent opponents from penetrating the defensive curtain unchallenged and to fill in for any central back momentarily drawn out of position. Deployed other than rigidly, he may become a creative defender and even, when the opportunity occurs, a powerfully supportive attacker.

During the sixties, as no-risk soccer began to dominate the international scene, forwards decreased in numbers until they were limited to three, often two and occasionally only one.

Unsupported, but expected to provide a secure outlet for the relief of his own besieged defenders, a lone striker must receive and hold the ball, under the most severe pressure, until players break out of deep defense to link up with him. They may be reluctant to do so especially having been under attack for some time.

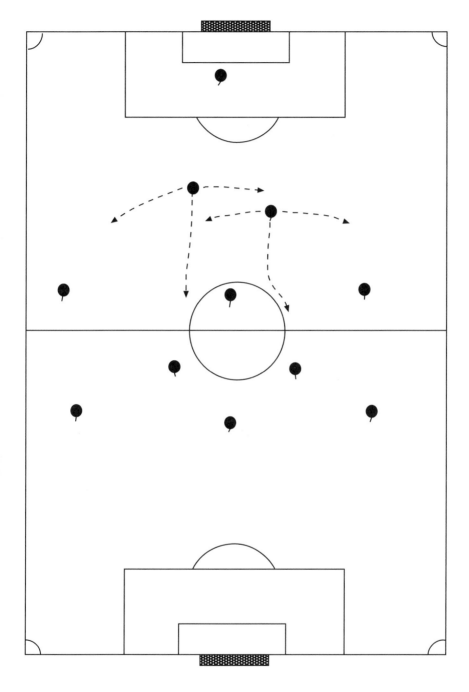

**Diagram 20.** Argentina's twin sweeper's.

'Cause and effect' is important in the evolution of soccer tactics. The deployment of a single, isolated striker required to hold the ball and make the most out of nothing much, produced a new breed. Small, athletic, mobile players with excellent control and wide vision emerged: players able to make the most of very little. High in their operational priorities was responsibility for 'dislocating' defensive organization by 'pulling' central defenders out of position. Most developed uncanny appreciations of areas where, at any given time, defenders least wanted to be; all this under the most punishing often illegal physical pressure.

Tactics were devised to prevent central dislocation and the role of the picket player was evolved. England's master strategist, Alf Ramsey, returned from a South American tour in 1964 having seen Argentina set enormous problems by employing a picket player in front of central defenders. Part of Ramsey's attacking strategy was to allow Bobby Charlton to penetrate opposing defenses with long runs from his self-chosen position left of centre in England's mid-field. Ramsey didn't want Charlton to defend but Bobby saw himself as a 'do-everything', traditional, English, mid-field play maker. From defending positions, Charlton was encouraged to move forward at speed, with or without the ball, to penetrate central defense disrupted by the split forward runs of strikers Hurst and Hunt. Argentina filled any 'hole' so created with a picket player who marked Charlton or anyone else trying to enter it.

The picket player patrols the shaded area diagram 21, to cut the lines of passes to the feet of any central attacker moving away from and to the side of central markers. He also reduces the effectiveness of any striker who drops deep to draw defense away from a more advanced team mate. Late, undetected runs by supporting players from deep positions go undetected no longer.

Threatening the lines of passes aimed for central attackers forces those players to move wider or deeper than they would wish. In addition, they are subjected to tackles from behind and interceptions or harassment from the side. In the event of the central marker being drawn very wide, diagram 21, this front sweeper or picket player fills that player's central position to pick up any other player trying to attack the space created by the central attacker's wide run. Additionally, if the sweeper has been drawn over to cover the threat of a wide break-through, the picket player drops back, temporarily, into the back sweeper role.

Rotation attacking play, or whirling play as it is was called by its initiator, Austrian Willy Meisl, requires almost constant movement of a large number of players into, through and out of the key attacking areas. Central backs cannot afford to follow the moves of opponents when threats posed by those moves may be partly real and partly a 'con'. The sweeper behind and the picket player in front of the back defensive curtain, are able to cover limited areas, allowing other defenders to mark tightly.

Reference was made earlier to an unusual deployment of double sweepers and to the price to be paid for two defenders free from marking commitments. Any defensive organization which has one free player behind and one in front of the marking backs must pay a price somewhere else on the pitch. There must be 'extra'

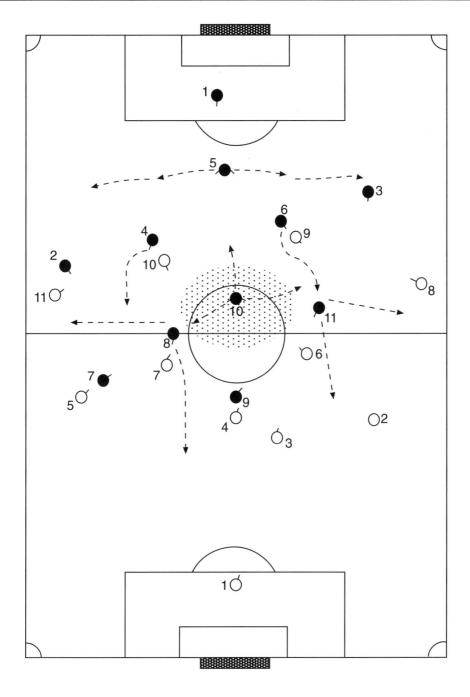

**Diagram 21.** The picket player, Black 10.

opponents somewhere who are not marked; if they think and act positively they will cause trouble.

'Free' backs must be encouraged to move forward in support of mid-field playing developments to allow the regular mid-field players to move further forward, even as out and out attackers.

## 4.18 Off-Side Tactics.

In some parts of the world, not least in English professional soccer, the off-side law has been used to compress play into very tight areas thereby threatening the effectiveness of individually skillful players, some might say their very existence; I would be one such person.

Skillful soccer needs the time and the space. . . the same thing really. . . to permit an extra touch to the ball or to gain that extra split second in which to assess options for clever play. Imaginative, deceptive players, players with sensitive touch, cannot always be 'instant' players. They need time in which to 'set up' opponents for skillful, penetrative thrusts.

Nevertheless, off-side tactics are legitimate, and they must be scrutinized carefully if they are to be defeated. First, off-side tactics give cover a low priority; they depend upon the willingness of back players to take risks by committing themselves completely to positions at least level with all advanced attackers. From these square positions and with split second timing they move forward as one to catch attackers offside as the forward pass is made.

The change in the off-side law allowing attackers to be level with the first of the required two 'last' defenders, assuming the second to be the goalkeeper, diagram 22, has made offside tactics so much more risky. Referees, increasingly, give 'the benefit of doubt' to attackers, as they always should.

Carried to the extremes, as it has been, off side play is really negative play. At least that's my opinion.

Soccer is about playing to win by scoring as many goals as possible. Negative tactics inspired by professional coaches lacking imagination and practiced by professional players lacking real skill must be made unprofitable.

Even so, offside tactics are still part of the game.

As opposing attacking play develops, advanced attackers may move back, to link up with mid-field play perhaps. If so, the whole back line moves with them. Opposing mid-field players, marked and denied space to turn with the ball, are compelled to pass to their own back players. The backs, with passage through mid-field blocked, have little choice other than to hit passes over the mid-field 'log jam' up to or beyond their forwards, diagram 23.

The waiting line of backs, deployed tightly up against advanced attackers, moves forward as one, leaving one or more attackers off-side. The backs' movement forward needs to be no more than five or six yards but it needs to be quick. Attackers caught off-side will be clearly seen even by linesmen suffering from less than 20:20 vision.

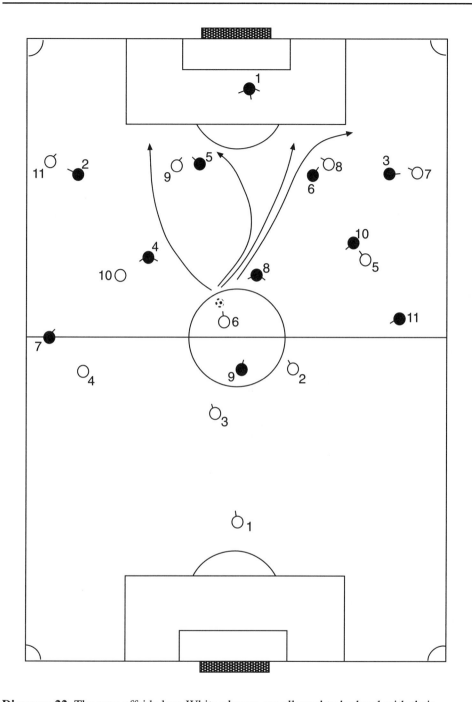

**Diagram 22.** The new offside law. White players are allowed to be level with their opponents.

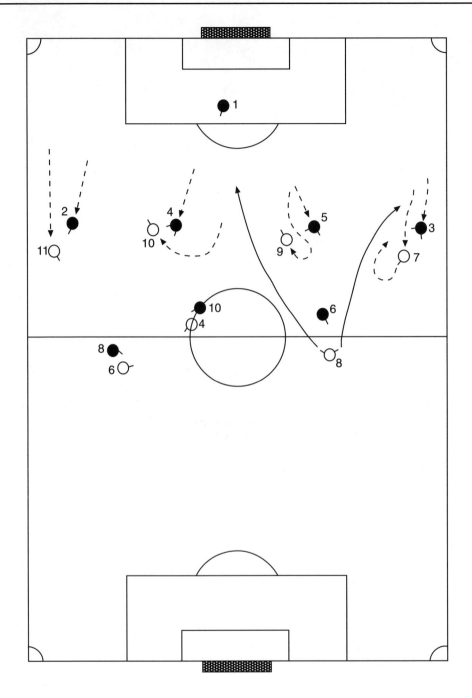

**Diagram 23.** Spinning to beat the offside trap.

To beat the trap, one or more attackers may move with the forward move of the defenders and, fractionally after the ball has been played, spin quickly into the space behind the backs, diagram 23. It's not as easy as it sounds but it is worth a lot of practice. Even if the spin is successful, the attacker with the ball is catchable by reasonably quick defenders without it.

The flat trap safety is improved if one player is positioned slightly in front and on the far side of the back line, diagram 24. He watches for any attacker turning late to collect the ball or moving forward from a deep position when he 'drops off' the back line into a covering position towards goal. Irrespective of whether the attacker is given off-side or not, his retreat must coincide with the ball's release. His starting position in front of his backs ensures that he does not interfere with the off-side trap. If off-side is given, all well and good, if not his move, almost certainly, positions him to deal with the danger anyway, diagram 24.

Ordinarily, an off-side trap is best controlled by the 'far-side' full-back when passes are aimed diagonally across the field into space behind the centre backs. The other backs press forward into tight marking positions and on the controller's signal they all move forward to spring the trap. In some teams, the back line moves back slightly towards their own goal as the opponent with the ball sets himself for the pass, thereby encouraging attackers to move in the same direction. . . which most are anxious to do anyway.

The controller is the player who, if the trap has been mistimed and an opponent is on-side, must drop back to recover the position by containing the player with the ball until other defenders have also recovered defensive positions. Tactically it will pay if the off-side controller is also the fastest defender available.

Off-side tactics are not really compatible with the deployment of a sweeper. His whole reason for being 'free' is to collect or to deter forward passes behind back defenders.

## 4.19 Doubling Up.

All players should have a working understanding of defensive principles and of accepted defensive priorities. Some will be strong in certain aspects of defensive play, not so strong in others perhaps.

Full backs, however, must master all defensive skills and the defensive tactics which those techniques are used to implement. Occasionally a full-back will face an opponent who poses unusual problems. He may have outstanding speed, exceptional dribbling skills, unusual height, superior agility and so on.

The back alone may not be able to control that opponent in all circumstances. Another player may be called upon to 'double up' against the attacker. The regular back may become the 'first' defender, marking the opponent tightly, while the player 'doubling up' becomes the second defender and offers immediate challenge should the first defender be beaten. Sometimes the players take station the other way round and the doubling up player becomes the first defender, it depends upon their respective playing strengths and weaknesses. The most important consideration when

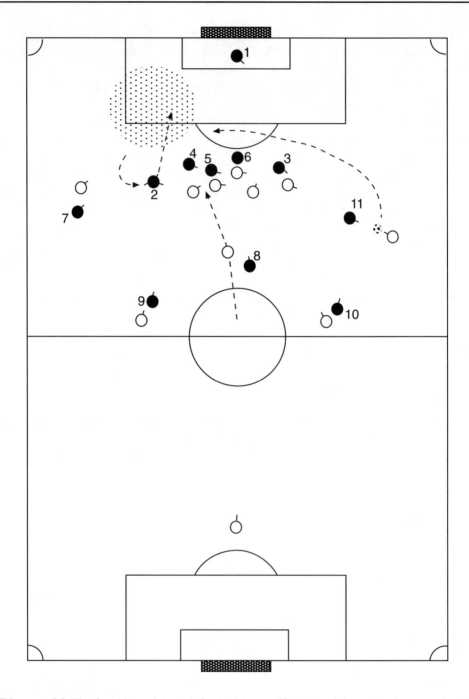

**Diagram 24**. The far-side, quickest defender 'drops off' late to pick up attackers moving to beat the offside trap.

doubling up effectively is for both players to know what each is trying to do.

The first defender must reduce the attacker's action options to as few as possible. The angle and speed of his approach to the attacker will show which option he will try to compel the attacker to take. The closer he is to the attacker and the more aggressive his controlling movements, the greater the likelihood that the first defender will tackle for the ball. If so the second defender provides cover and defensive concentration 'just in case'. Where the first defender allows his opponent some freedom of movement he indicates where and how he intends 'jockeying' (maneuvering) that opponent into the most disadvantageous position. The second defender needs to be vigilant since the attacker may have enough room to try for a different option.

In diagram 25 (a) the full-back, black 2, has taken up the first defending position in front of the doubling up player, black 8. He needs to give the opponent a limited opportunity to move in one direction only, in this example onto his weaker foot which, let's say, is his 'inside' or right foot. The first defender's angle of approach to the attacker will be to deny him any reasonable chance of moving down the touchline, i.e. onto his good foot. Black 2 has offered the attacker the inside option. Even so, the defender will work for a position as close to the attacker as he can. The further away he is the less the control he has over the attacker's actions. The second defender, knowing what the full-back's tactics are, positions himself on an inside angle near enough to present an immediate challenge should the attacker try to break through 'inside' and towards goal.

Confronted with the threat from a dribbler of outstanding talent, able to beat defenders on the inside or outside, in almost no space at all, the second defender may double up on the outside angle, diagram 25 (b), thereby offering the attacker no space whatsoever for an outside break.

Doubling up and containing opponents to restrict their options is a matter of angle of approach, angle of cover, distance to the opponent and distance between the first and the second defender, plus the speed of decision and action.

All full-backs. . . indeed all defending players. . . must learn how to maneuver or . . . as it is known in England. . . 'jockey' opponents towards preferred areas and away from dangerous ones.

It cannot be overstressed that, when defending, clear and positive communication between players is vital. Defending players worry most about what they cannot see. Unable to see and lacking information, defenders become uncertain and nervous. Uncertainty is removed when one player takes responsibility for directing other defenders confidently by keeping them informed about activity behind them. Good players know what is happening in any part of the field, especially behind them, but in the sometimes hectic action which defending close to goal involves, the rearmost defenders may not have much time to look.

The backs should control the defensive activity of players in the first defensive curtain. Defenders in the front curtain need to know when and how far to push forward onto opposing attackers: when and how far to drop back: when to pick up

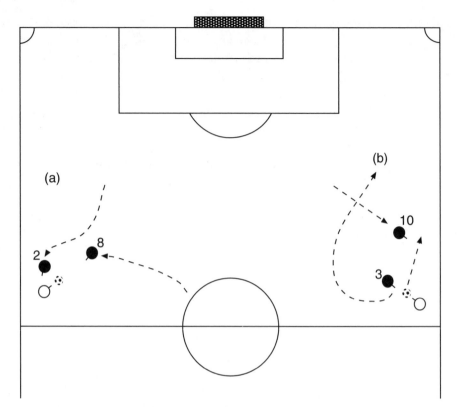

**Diagram 25 (a) and (b)**. Doubling up defenders position themselves to limit an opponent's options.

attackers stealing through the defense from deep positions: when to tackle or when to hold off and so on. When defenders in the front curtain are doing their work properly, the backs find defending easy. Passes delivered up to the strikers will be hurried and to that extent lacking in the quality so helpful to a pass receiver. Pass receivers will not have the time in which to use decoy moves to prepare to receive passes in advantageous situations.

Most forward passes will be at the convenience of the passer and not, as they should be, for the convenience of the receiver. Passers will find normal lines of sight to target players blocked by defenders' bodies. Where first defenders make opponents accept the ball facing their own goal and compel them to play passes backwards, passes subsequently played to forwards are likely to be too long, too high, too hurried and too obvious. Defending backs should pick these passes off easily and all day! And there speaks a former centre back!

### 4.20 Deflecting attackers.
Controlling opponents and compelling them to play in an unfamiliar way or a way not of their choosing is a most. . . perhaps THE most. . . important tactical skill which a team, an individual or a group of players within a team, can have.

Successful defensive strategies aim. . among other things. . . to deflect opponents' play into parts of the field which are disadvantageous to them. Opponents must be prevented from playing to their strengths. Complementary to that aim is the need to deflect opposing attacking play away from a defending team's weaknesses.

Reference has been made already to deflection methods e.g. by jockeying individual players away from goal to positions outside the defensive structure. The wide full-backs, mid-field players or wing attackers, depending how a team deploys its players, are often the targets for defensive clearance play. The opposing full-backs are often the first players positioned to exert directional control over attacking play. They can either jockey opponents towards outside options or, by blocking outside options they can force play along 'inside' lines, diagram 25. They may choose the latter for various  reasons. Their central defenders or the goalkeeper may not be confident when dealing with crosses pulled back from the goal-line. Central mid-field defense may be very strong; advantage may be gained from making opponents attack there. Alternatively, where a defending side is losing by, say, one goal with little playing time left, inside deflection may give defending mid-field players chances to intercept passes and to initiate effective counter-attack in centre field. That's where, given space, counter attack really hurts.

Tactically, a losing team needs play to be open if they are to have a chance of scoring. Where play is contained in tight areas, especially in the opponents' half of the pitch, it will be to the advantage of the team already winning.

The techniques of deflecting and containing are simple. They don't demand any particular degree of courage. . . as in tackling perhaps. . but they do demand careful thought and sustained application. But then, so do all aspects of the game of it is to be played well.

## 4.21 Man marking or zonal marking.

Strict man to man marking is worthwhile when defending players are aggressively confident that each can master the opponent for whom he has responsibility. Mastering an opponent means that the marking player must be confident of success in controlling that opponent in the various ways at his disposal: by out-running him, by tackling him, by intercepting passes aimed for him and so on. When unable to tackle or intercept, the marker must be sure that he and not the attacker determines the attackers' options. Finally, a marker's control of his opponent must allow the marker to make reasonable contributions to his team's counter attacking play.

That's how individual defensive mastery should be judged. Team tactics may require a specific marking task to be carried out on an opponent without attempting the total mastery referred to earlier. For example, the marker's task may be to ensure that a particular opponent only plays the ball when facing his own goal. That player may be much more effective when he has the opposing goal in sight, particularly when a shooting chance is in the offing. Players like that demand special attention. When full-backs are given man to man marking tasks the marked players will determine to a great extent where those markers play. Clever attackers, marked tightly, try to draw their markers away from positions in which those markers can make contributions to collective defense. In effect they are saying, "You may mark me out of the game but I'll take you out of it as well".

Obviously the greater the number of players given strict man marking responsibilities, the less predictable the roles which those markers can fulfill in team based defense.

In these circumstances, a sweeper is absolutely essential and a picket player or front sweeper, only marginally less so. These two players will block dangerous situations in central defense and fill any dangerously exposed spaces as will arise from time to time.

I recall newly appointed German Bundes Coach, Jupp Derwall, asking which it should be, 'man deckung oder raum deckung'. Man marking or space (zone) marking.

Space marking or zonal defense, in the strictest sense, is founded upon defenders' abilities to anticipate directional changes in attack and thereby to contract and expand the distance relationships between each other as and when required. In practice, space filling defenders are only effective when they compel opponents to interpass and move, with or without the ball, outside the defensive structure and at a safe distance from goal. Any opposing player attempting to move inside the defense must be marked very tightly indeed. So the answer to Jupp Derwall's question had to be, 'It depends.'

Players are much more important than space, irrespective of where that space is. Space only becomes a problem when attackers move into it unopposed. Even in a professional team heavily committed to attack, it would be rare to see that team equal the defending team numerically in the last quarter of the field, except at free kicks and corner kicks.

A defending team is certain to have at least eight or nine players, sometimes all of them, compressing the final attacking quarter. Clearly that team can mark key opponents tightly on a man to man basis and deploy players to fill the important spaces as well. Unless. . . unless their opponents are prepared to deploy an equal number of players in attacking positions.

**One day they may. . . I hope!**

# Chapter 5
# Back Play - Attack

Tactics involving full-backs in all phases of attack are relatively new in the game's evolution. When the roles and the functions of backs, half-backs and forwards were fairly rigidly defined, a full-back was expected to get the ball and give it. . . quickly. . . to more skillful players in mid-field. Their only other option was to kick it into the far distance or out of play. Only half-backs and inside forwards set up counter attacking play. Mid-field players were the game's skilled craftsmen: forwards were the game's finishers, full-backs were second class citizens almost, the game's laborers.

Times and functions have changed. Full backs now, wide or central, are expected to integrate skillfully and comfortably in all phases of play. . . at least in forward looking countries they are!

## 5.1  Counter Attack.

Counter attack differs from attack in that it occurs as an immediate response to an attack from the opposing team. . . or it should. Normal attacking play need not be governed by any sense of urgency: counter attack is. The distinction may seem to be hardly worth making but in play it certainly is.

If, when a team regains possession, a large number of players moves into forward positions effective passing options, through, over and behind their opponents will be created and shooting opportunities will be more likely, quite often within a few passes.

The speed of counter attack will be determined by:

(a) the speed at which target players take up advanced positions.

(b) the degree to which those players are within range of the passing skills of the pass makers.

(c) the 'vision' of  pass makers.

(d) the time it takes pass makers to deliver the ball. This is a measure of the touch and accuracy of the pass makers' skills. . . all of them!

On the other hand, when mounting an attack, a team may take time to maneuver for positions because the opposing team may be well organized and fully deployed in  defense.

Counter attack is designed to catch the opposing team off-balance through skill applied deceptively at speed.

In a straight forward attacking situation, that isn't necessarily so .

## 5.11 Running the Ball.

Many years ago a myth was spawned in English professional soccer that the best (only) way to move the ball out of deep defense was to pass it or, worse, to kick it, as far as possible! Full backs of the time were, by selection, muscularly well endowed but severely limited technically so they chose to pass (or kick) the ball safely and thereby predictably. Everyone knew when and where they would pass which simplified life for opponents, substantially.

When exposed technically a pass back to the goalkeeper saved most backs from the ultimate embarrassment of being caught in possession of the ball. However, when FIFA stopped goalkeepers from handling back passes, many backs were in real trouble. Unable to pass deceptively: unable to hold the ball confidently: unable to dribble the ball out of trouble; lacking the touch to bring a ball under control instantly, or sooner, their only option was to kick the ball hard and anywhere. Rather than being used to get backs out of trouble, most interpassing attempts only put them in trouble. . . deep in it ! And yet, occasionally, the most surprising move of all for a full-back to take is to run the ball. If he is decisive often he will find himself comfortably past even those opponents inclined to defend; occasionally he will find himself past opposing mid-field players as well.

He needs to know two things:

(a) when and where to release the ball in the interests of further progress and

(b) that someone has moved to cover him should a mistake occur.

German full-backs are very good at running the ball at and past opponents. These tactics reflect the blitzkrieg attacking attitudes that Germans favor in all competitive activities. 'Weiter immer weiter,' (onwards ever onwards) is their creed.

Berti Vogts, recently national team coach,and in his time Germany's supreme 'defensive enforcer',  marked opponents so tightly that he came off the field wearing their after shave. Having won the ball, Vogts was quick to seize chances to run the ball deep at the heart of an opposing team. He would give and take return passes with anyone to get forward. Hans-Pieter Briegel, was a German world class left back in the same 'panzer player' mold and Andreas Brehmer was another off the same assembly line. Paul Breitner was an all-time world great in the same position. It doesn't happen by chance; it comes from careful selection and rigorous education and practice.

To run the ball a full-back needs space in which to begin his run, then he needs space through which he can continue safely. In diagram 26, where black 4 has the ball forty yards from his goal, he can't run it into the space in front of him; an opponent, white 10, is too close. To gain momentum, black 4 will have to dribble the ball to one side or the other and past his opponent. Additionally, he can only pass to negatively positioned colleagues, each one of whom is likely to be under pressure quickly, certainly too quickly for comfort. And dribbling the ball is not the same as running it strongly.

To dribble effectively a player has to be clever at manipulating the ball. Being clever is a matter of touch and movement deceptiveness rather than strength. A dribbling player may be more easily dispossessed by a tackle than when he is running the ball strongly.

In diagram 26, if the ball is passed to the other backs they will be no better placed to run it than black 4. Relatively short, positional adjustments by opponents will contain them easily.

In diagram 27, the black backs have exaggerated their forward and backward positions thereby making opponents move up and down the pitch rather than sideways, to contain them. Psychologically, players aren't inclined to move forward to contain an opponent only to see him pass the ball behind them.

In a twin centre back formation, it is so much easier for three attackers to contain them. In diagram 26 where there is a free back, notice how much safer the situation is and how much greater are the options open to them. If the worst comes to the worst, the libero is always available to get another back out of trouble. He is also the player who can most readily start trouble. . . for the opposing team.

The backs push forward or pull back exaggerating their positional relationships to make space and to test the determination of opponents to contain them. If the opposing forwards are determined in their containment efforts, the backs may have to interchange positions quicker and more fluidly, in all directions.

Where one of the backs attacks towards and possibly through mid-field, mid-field players must make space for him, diagram 26. At the same time they may offer themselves as supporting (interpassing) players. By moving, they increase available space whether they are followed or not. If they are followed by markers then the space created will be free temporarily of any interference. If the mid-field players make their 'space clearance' moves wide and backwards, in a circular pattern, and time the moves shrewdly, they will be able to cover any mistakes should the backs get into difficulties.

Opposing defenders now have difficult problems. How far dare they follow their mid-field opponents' circular movements? When should they desert their marking responsibility to block the run of the full-back for instance? When they slacken their marking of an opposing mid-field player, will he be able to set up even more penetrative, interpassing moves with his team mate?

These problems take us back to the question and answer approach to developing soccer intelligence. Players who pose questions to which there are a number of answers, each of which may be wrong, are on their ways to becoming exceptional players in any company.

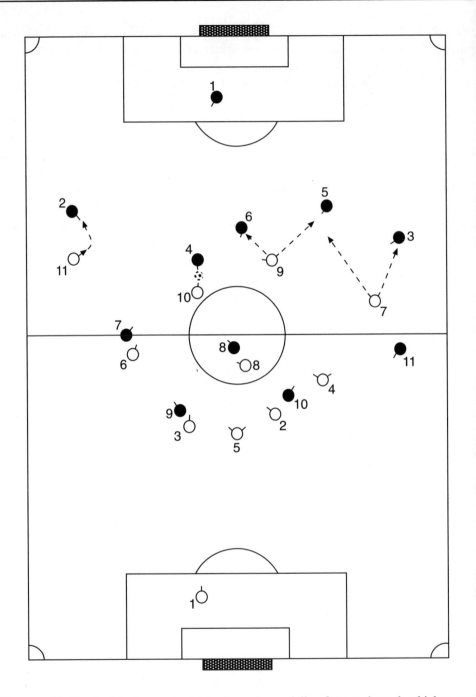

**Diagram 26.** The denial of space to the backs and especially of space through which to run the ball.

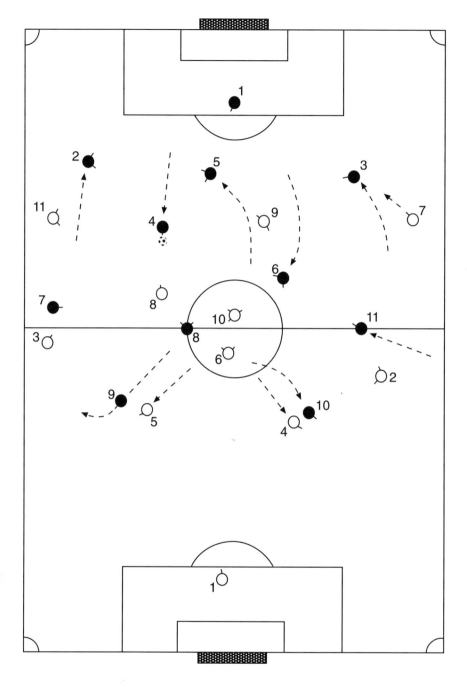

**Diagram 27.** Exaggerating positional relationships to set marking problems for opponents.

Circular (rotational) movements by players in front of the ball, diagram 28, aimed at drawing opposing markers away from the spaces needed by attackers, must be practiced and understood by all teams which aspire to defeat the combined space filling and man marking methods used in modern, top-class soccer.

When running the ball, in principle a player has three options, he can run the ball at the nearest defender's left side, at his right or straight at him. If the defender is marking another opponent so much the better. If the player with the ball takes none of the three options almost certainly he's going nowhere of immediate importance.

The effects of the positive choices are important.

Someone, clearly, must resist the attacker's run. Where a back has another opponent to mark and if that player pulls away from his marker when the ball runner is, say, five or six yards away, the defender is in double jeopardy. If he follows his immediate opponent, the ball runner moves past him towards goal. If he challenges the ball runner, black 5, he may be beaten by an interpassing move between black 5 and black 10 in diagram 29. Alternatively the player with the ball may dribble the ball past him anyway.

If the full-back runs the ball at space to the side of a blocking defender, that defender must move over to challenge the run. When he does so, any other attacker quick to show himself in the space vacated is likely to increase the probability of penetration by one or the other of the attacking players.

If the interpassing option is not needed, the player offering it can look for another position in advance of the ball or, if he feels that the team 'shape' has been left unbalanced and exposed to possible counter-attacks, he can circle behind the attacking back, temporarily assuming that player's responsibilities.

## 5.12 Controlling Possession of The ball in Attack.

Full backs often receive the ball from goal-keeper throw-outs, or they should. Initial attacking play must be established on player deployments from which final assaults on goal are probable. The speed of attack isn't as important as control and accuracy because the opposing team may have had time to re-form defensively. Speed of attack isn't necessarily important but variation in the speed of attack certainly is, as we shall see later.

In diagram 30 (a) the ball is in the possession of the wide back, black 3. He has the passing options shown by the arrowed lines. This is NOT a situation in which to run the ball! The players are deployed in the English twin centre back system and the two strikers, white 8 and 9, with assistance from white 11, should contain their opponents fairly easily. If they don't contain them, their presence will deter most central backs from getting involved in risky build-up play. Passing back to the goalkeeper recently ceased to be a major option and not before time!

The situation is improved immeasurably if a free back is available. In a well organized team a central attacker could move to contain the free back, diagram 30 (b), but three attackers can't contain every back player where there are five of them. Another attacker would have to be pushed forward to create a four on five situation.

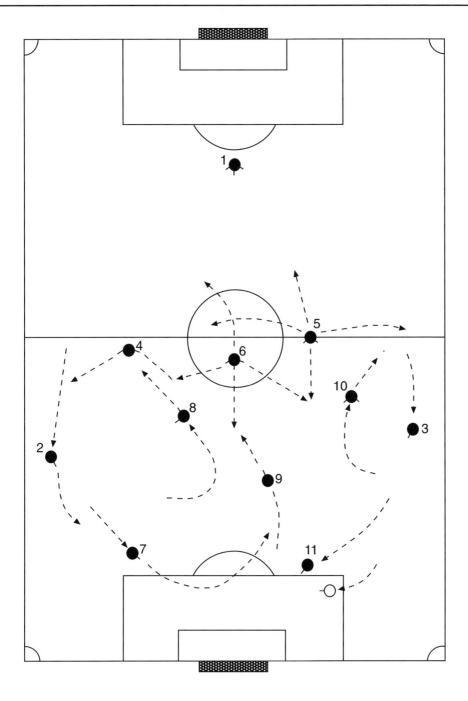

**Diagram 28.** Rotational or circular movement patterns designed to liberate space in attacking play.

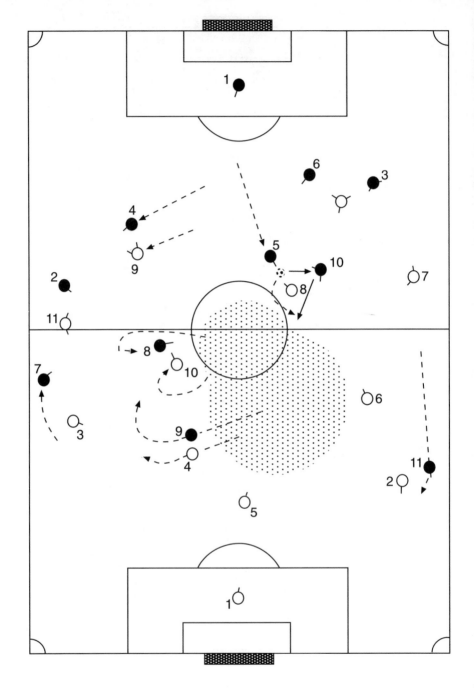

**Diagram 29**. Setting up a defender for double jeopardy moves.

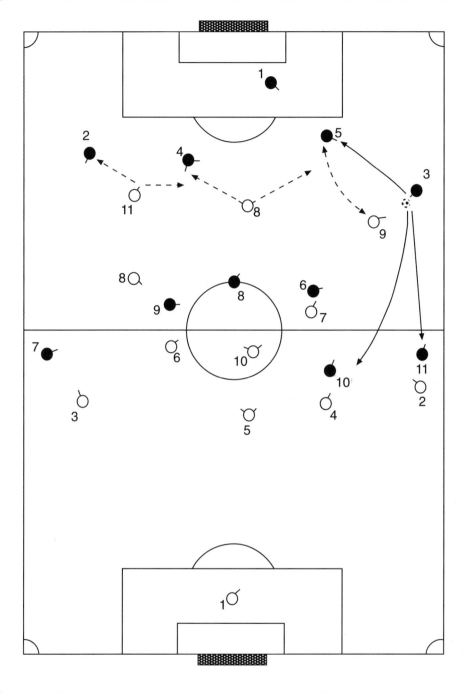

**Diagram 30 (a).** Splitting four backs with three to contain full-back play.

**Diagram 30 (b)**. Passing options created by the introduction of a free back.

It sounds sensible enough and is but not a lot of ultra cautious, modern teams would care to take the risk, a risk which is more imaginary than real. More importantly, the left full-back, with the ball, can consider different interpassing options knowing that if a slip up occurs, the libero can rescue the position.

The use of the libero to free attacking play illustrates perfectly the need, in ALL phases of attacking play, for an extra player. Diagram 31. He is the element which makes variation in attacking play possible. He can force opponents into errors. Without the extra player, forcing opponents into errors becomes very hard work or needs guaranteed player to player superiority.

**The higher the class of soccer, the more difficult it is to guarantee anything.**

Soccer isn't played by rigidly observing certain 'do's and don'ts'. Played well, it relies on versatility and variability based upon sound principles; nevertheless if a team expects certain moves to occur, with reasonable confidence, then the unexpected is more likely to succeed.

In principle, no player should receive the ball without reasonable support immediately at hand unless that player has total superiority over his immediate opponent. If having made a pass, other than a long one, the passing player moves towards the receiving player and even past him, two purposes are served; first, the receiver knows that at least one player will support him; second, the movements by themselves cause fluid interchanges of position. Diagram 32. If supporting movements are continuous, effective rotational play can be a likely consequence and that has to be in the game's best interests.

Players with the wit and appearance of marble statues play like marble statues: immovably.

Generally speaking, where backs play for position. . . to move the ball securely into the opponents' half of the field say. . . they pass to the feet of pass receivers. If they pass into space, for the receiver to move onto, they must be one hundred and ten percent certain that there is no chance of an opponent interception. This does not mean that the backs cannot interpass to move the ball past opponents. Not all strikers are prepared to defend against well executed inter-passing moves.

Surprise is a basic principle of attacking play but an extension to it is that the greater the surprise sought for, the further away from its own goal a team needs to be.

**Never dirty your own doorstep!**

Defenders involved in interplay should ensure that at least one 'fail safe' player is nearby. Opponents cannot be sure if the interpassing move will continue and if so, how far. These moves, to be absolutely successful, require unusual interchanges of position and the movements of other backs to balance them. Most interpassing moves between the backs in today's soccer are merely moves to transfer the ball to

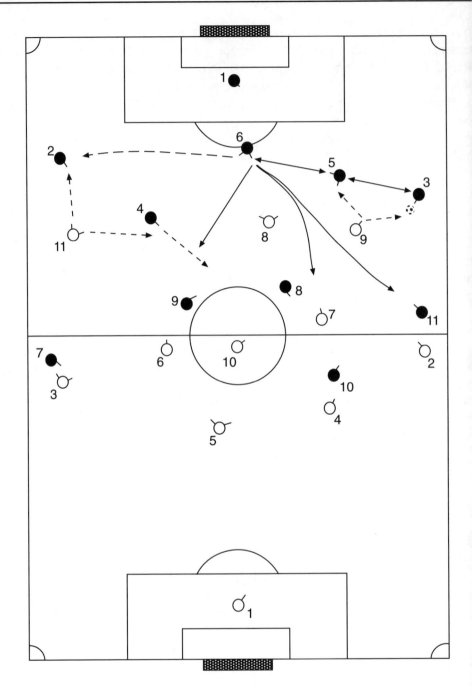

**Diagram 31.** The liberating effect of a free back on attacking play by the backs.

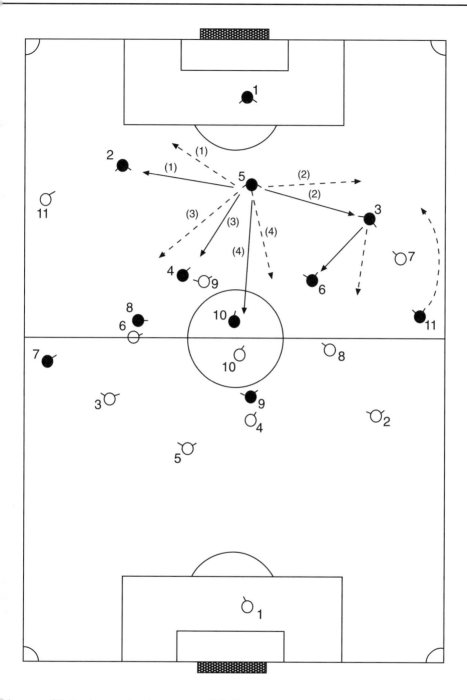

**Diagram 32.** Backs moving in support of their own passes.

mid-fielders, to strikers or across the field to each other.

In intelligent, sophisticated teams, positive interpassing between backs, especially where a libero and a picket player are involved, becomes the basis for all attacking movements. The possibilities for launching deceptive, accurate and variably paced assaults on goal are limitless. Predictable soccer is boring soccer and is more a reflection of the lack of imagination among coaches than upon the willingness and skill of players. Players enjoy skillful risk taking. Don't we all?

Where the player most likely to receive a pass in space and beyond, say, the first curtain of defense is a back, that player will be encouraged to move forward when he is confident that his defensive role and position has been covered by another player. Balance and team shape are important considerations in the game. It might be simpler and safer perhaps for a back to run the ball past opponents but interpassing is an option which, for the sake of variety and therefore of surprise, must be considered.

The main reason why backs do not (are not permitted to) contribute more to attacking play is because coaches fear risk and discourage players from practicing such moves.

Where a professional team dare not undertake certain moves among, say, the backs, because the coach feels that his players lack the basic skill to execute the moves successfully, the question has to be asked, "Just what do the players and the coach do with all the time at their disposal."

When forward pressing opponents prevent attacking play developing from the back and through mid-field, accurate passes from the backs over mid-field to the forwards may be necessary, as an option.

It is important to avoid making presents of passes to interceptors. There are two possibilities:

First, the passer shows every intention to pass to the feet of a striker moving someway to meet it. His actual pass is played over both striker and marker into space behind them.

Alternatively the passer shows his intention to pass into space behind the striker and his marker. His actual pass is played as low as possible through mid-field or over it making reception by the target player as easy as possible at no more than knee height. Long passes over opponents can be very effective it used occasionally accurately and with an element of surprise. Surprise is improved when another player actually moves for the fake pass.

Long, obvious passes encourage losing and painful confrontations between strikers and their markers; they are a waste of effort, everyone's. Their strongest advocates usually have had no personal experience of the pain of the resultant aerial dog fights.

I listened with disbelief to an international team manager, himself a former player, screaming at his central striker to 'hold it' (the ball) when the target player was having to sprint ten yards and take off into his highest possible jump to make any sort of contact with the ball at all. What he was supposed to hold the ball with was never nade clear. Passes were rifled at the striker from all of fifty-yards away and his marker enjoyed hitting both him and the ball. . . often in that order. . . painfully and egularly.

Passes played over mid-field should be targeted at areas into which the receiver an move at a time and speed to suit himself. He, after all, has the problem of maneuvering one or more opponents in other directions before committing himself to eceive the pass.

In diagram 33, where the striker can see that the full-back, black 5, has poor nterpassing options, the striker quickly assesses how much pressure his team mate aces. If there appears to be no desperation he may draw his marker away from the nost likely line of a long pass which is towards the shaded area. The full-back should leliver the ball with as little 'weight' as possible so that as it drops into the target area t 'dies' and presents few controlling problems to the receiver. Black 10 (and black 9) noves away from the expected target area, keeping one eye on the passer while sensng the movement of his marker. When the pass is 'on' the striker may throw a very juick fake move before moving smoothly into the target area to receive the ball. It is only through practiced co-ordination of the two players' actions, real and false, that he striker can move to the ball without the close and painful attendance of a narker and with a good chance of gaining advantageous possession of the ball. In liagram 33, the second striker seeing that the required pass isn't excessively long nay execute a second 'dummy run' before spinning back into a receiving position oeyond his team mate black 10.

Knowing precisely what your team mates' capabilities are is even more important han having the same insight into the capabilities of your opponents.

Long forward passes from the backs should either be played into pre-arranged target areas which allow the receiver to move at an angle to collect them or into a target area along a line which is at an angle to the receiver's starting position. Diagram 3. In both cases an angled pass allows the attacker to receive the ball to some extent urned towards the direction which he wishes to take AND in a position to make ome judgment of his opponents' intentions, particularly those of his marker. A long oass played along the same line down which the receiver must run to receive it, nevitably invites an all out tackling challenge from a marker usually through the oass receiver. Whatever the marker does he can't lose.

Even if the striker controls the ball and turns it behind his opponent, the striker is inlikely to be allowed to follow it. . . if you know what I mean!

## .13 Exploiting Defensive Holes.

deally, strikers prefer the ball to be played to them along the ground: not always easy or a full-back, but not impossible. It's the mid-field players who can make this oossible; they must understand that only one of them should seek pass receiving oositions himself. Where the opposing mid-field unit is heavily committed to liminating their opponents, this can be to the advantage of full-backs seeking to leliver the ball directly to the strikers or into space nearby.

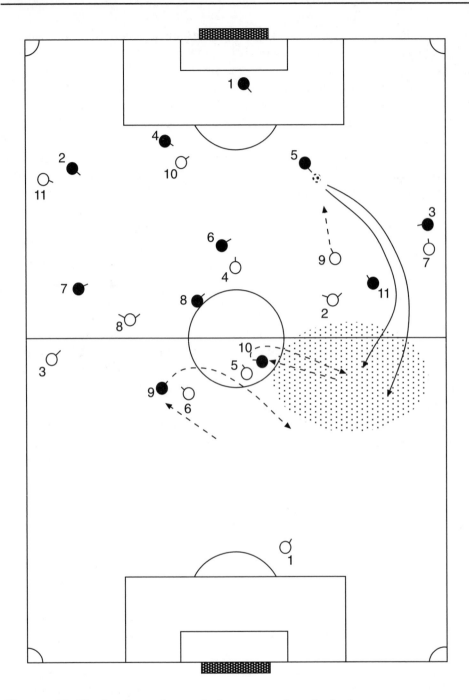

**Diagram 33.** Clearing forward space for long passes from the backs.

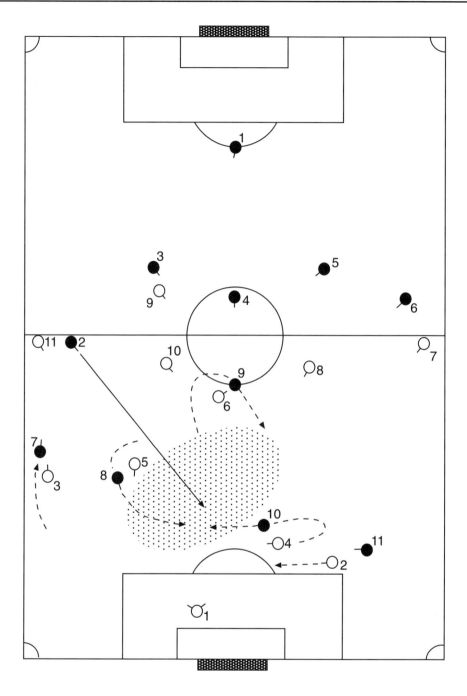

**Diagram 34.** Creating holes in defenses for penetrating passes.

Mid-field opponents marked tightly, man-to-man, take their opponents with them wherever they go. Making space for themselves will be difficult; making space between themselves and other players will be a good deal easier. When mid-field players see a full-back with the time to hit a decent forward pass, over thirty yards or so, they will draw their markers away from each other to expose a hole through which the pass can travel.

In diagram 34, two players near to the wide back, black 8 and 9, have pulled away from each other apparently looking for a pass. In fact they have opened up a hole for a forward pass to black 10. As the pass is made and in expectation of it, the mid-field players spin late and quickly around their markers to support the real target player.

If the ball is moved along the back line in the search for opportunities to pass it forward, diagram 35, mid-field players must close and open 'the holes', thereby giving direct access to forward players.

Mid-field markers will not be easily drawn to leave large holes in the first defensive curtain. If decoy opponents move too far too soon, markers will let them go while sustaining depth and cover. They will invite passes to the feet of the now widely positioned opponents and then close down against those opponents quickly as the pass is made. Moves to open the holes must be patient to ensure that markers are drawn as far away from each other as possible. The moves to make the holes must be timed to coincide with a back's readiness to pass. Full backs (and all other players for that matter) need to develop two footed skills: especially those for swerving passes with the outside of the foot and along the ground.

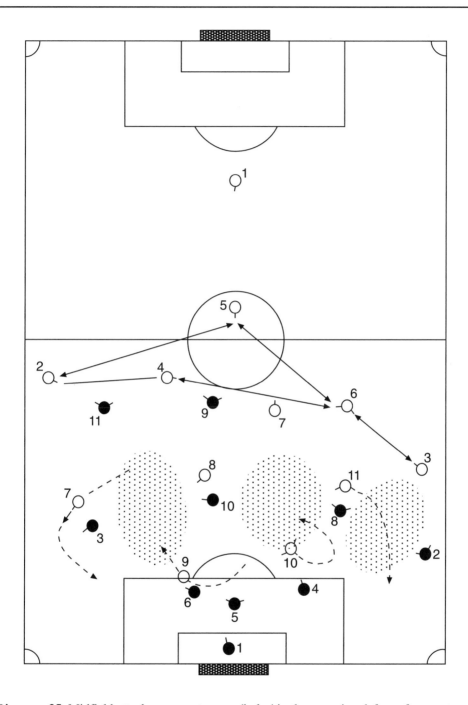

**Diagram 35.** Midfield attackers move to open 'holes' in the opposing defense for penetrating passes from the backs.

# Chapter 6
# Individual Tactical Skills

Tactics are arrangements made between two or more players to defeat opponents, in attack or defense. Often they are more effective than single, individual abilities are likely to be: often but by no means always.

Individual players, aware of their own technical, athletic and psychological strengths, (and deficiencies) will organize their personal tactics to make the most of those strengths and to hide weaknesses. Here are three examples.

(a) A central back can play well with his right foot but his left foot's value is mainly to prevent him falling down!

In the light of this deficiency he would be well advised to move to his right whenever he receives the ball. This maximizes the width of his passing angle on his 'good' foot, and includes as much of the field as possible. He should develop 'fake' moves left to draw opponents away from his preferred arc of play before changing back to his favored right.

He must avoid being jockeyed to his left, especially towards the left touch-line which, in effect, is another restriction on his arc of play. To turn inside and onto his better foot opens up a better passing angle but it also gives opponents time to read his intentions and intercept his pass. He must work for the optimum space in which to maneuver with his right foot when he needs to hold the ball.

This player's personal tactics will be to hide his left foot weakness by avoiding being forced to use it or by being jockeyed into limited areas down the left side of the field.

Team members who operate near to him must be aware of the various possibilities which different match conditions and opposing tactics impose on this player. Their positional options, wherever possible, must compensate for his weaknesses and support his strengths.

(b) A full-back, who is very skillful in possession of the ball and an outstanding supporter of attacking play, lacks speed and agility.

These are important deficiencies which if exposed will cause the whole defensive structure serious problems.

A slow back must position himself to contain opponents or to cover much earlier than quicker players. He must be acutely aware of the distances which develop between himself and immediate opponents and between himself and other backs. Team mates should position themselves so that their slower team mate is never isolated in one v one situations in space. Wherever possible a team mate should present himself as first defender against a threatening and speedier opponent.

The slow back must always assume that a threat to play a pass or to run for a pass behind him is real: more often than not it will be. A slow player cannot run the risk of an even race; he must always start first in any race for the ball so he must become a good judge of other players' intentions. This full-back, more than most, may allow or even encourage the ball to be passed between opponents in front of him. He does so to minimize any possibility of the ball being passed behind him. He may deliberately encourage inter-passing across his front and bank on his containing skill to control the situation. He certainly cannot afford to mark touch-tight because he always needs a few yards start whenever a race for the ball is likely.

In retreat or recovery a slow back must become extra skillful at judging the timing and the lines of opponents' passes so that he can cut across them to threaten interceptions, thereby making time to gain a better defensive position.

(c) My third example involves a full-back who lacks the mental toughness and physical commitment needed to be a hard-tackling defender. This player must learn to out-think opponents defensively.

Whenever his immediate opponent is a likely pass receiver, the back must be close enough early enough to prevent that opponent from turning with the ball. He must move frequently and quickly to achieve close if not touch-tight containing positions. If his opponent turns with the ball, the back must be close enough to 'poke' the ball away without having to tackle. Having achieved good containing positions, he can be taught that tackling an opponent who has been prevented from running at him at speed is not so difficult and painless.

A defender must move close enough to tackle before his opponent can gather any speed. Making a front block tackle is not a skill enjoyed by many players when an opponent is running at them head on and powerfully. The trick is to prevent opponents from gaining speed in the first place: it's called playing with the inside of your head not merely the outside.

Personal tactical skills involve the use of the game's techniques to optimum advantage. . . the where, the when, as well as the how of soccer.

## 6.1 Marking.

Marking an opponent is one of the most important defensive skills in the game and it isn't merely a matter of knowing where to stand in relation to an opponent. Marking involves constant adjustment of position, timing of movement and a great deal of cunning. . even acting at times.

The principles of good marking require:

(a) The marker to be positioned between his opponent and the marker's own goal.

(b) The marker to be touch-tight to his opponent. He must be able to reach out with his arm and touch his opponent without having to stretch to do so.

(c) The marker to be in a position which allows him to watch his opponent and any action with or near to the ball at the same time.

These three principles are stated in order of importance. Number one is more important than two and two more important than three.

**6.11 Positioning.**

By positioning himself between the goal and his opponent, the marker is able to threaten, immediately, any attempt by the attacker to turn with the ball. The marker may position himself slightly to one side of his opponent according to where the goal is behind them. An 'inside' marking position offers the attacker the option of turning outside and an outside marking position offers an inside turn. Both marking positions offer turning options which the marker will be prepared for. 'Outside' turns will be that much further to one side of the goal and set up a wider and more difficult shooting angle. Diagram 36.

Occasionally the back may mark to meet a particular condition or to deny his opponent certain playing options. For example, near to the touch-line a back normally tries to trap his opponent between himself and the line. If his team is

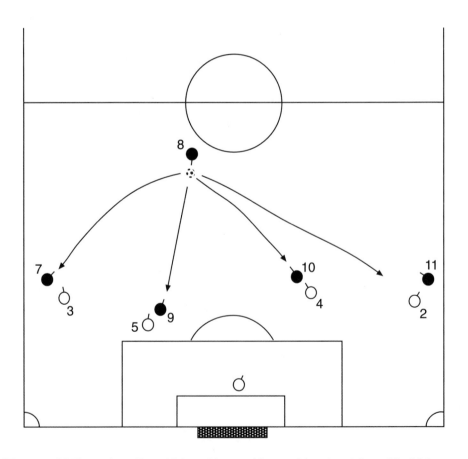

**Diagram 36.** Examples of 'outside' marking positions, whites 4 and 5: and 'inside' positions, whites 2 and 3.

losing late in the game say, the back may offer the opponent an inside turn which, while increasing his playing arc might enable the back to tackle successfully and thereby to open up immediate attacking and scoring opportunities. The nearer to goal, the more risky these tactics become, but there's a price to be paid for every- thing.

## 6.12  Touch-tight marking.

Touch-tight is as close as most circumstances in the game demand. It allows the marker to see around and past his opponent if the ball is passed towards him. This is necessary if an interception is an option.

If the defender doesn't intercept but holds a containing position, a touch-tight stance gives him some freedom of movement to 'work' his opponent without over-balancing. When 'working' an opponent the defender makes threatening moves to kick the ball away or to gain possession. He isn't merely content to wait for his opponent to make the first move. As a result of working his opponent, the back makes his opponent react to him rather than the other way round.

'Containing' and 'working' an opponent is the classic cat and mouse situation for full-backs. Most attackers dislike touch-tight marking intensely. Being compelled to occupy the same space as another player is annoying; it is intended to be!

Attackers subjected to persistent tight marking become desperate and run in any direction eventually to get away. They give more thought to getting away from their marker than to their responsibilities for fulfilling their tactical roles by seeking important positions to assist their team mates. When attackers, especially strikers, are forced to lose composure and run anywhere to escape, the marker has won an important tactical battle, the battle of minds.

## 6.13  Shirt tight marking.

Occasionally, backs face very clever players who require special attention if their tactical effectiveness is to be broken. These players are often easy moving, lazy looking players who play with unruffled composure, and not a hair on their heads out of place. They lay off the softest of passes or casually coax the ball, millimeter perfect, through impossible gaps for goals to be scored. These players seem to have all the time in the world and so they do. . . if defenders stand off and give it to them!

They may be less than 'cool' when marking is shirt tight: when the marker is no more than two or three inches away all the time, even when the ball is at the other end of the field.

Markers must be aware, however, that shirt tight marking can be used against them. A marker's choice of movement options will also be severely limited by an attacker so close to him. The marker will rarely have a good view of the ball; he will not be able to judge when to attack it, to intercept or tackle, as comfortably as he might like. The marker must learn how to press tightly against his opponent until at the last moment dropping back a few feet to give himself movement space and sight of the action in front of his opponent. By dropping 'off' no more then a couple of feet, the marker gives himself the space to readjust his position to intercept, tackle or to contain.

He must not be so close as to enable the marked player to lean back against him to use that position to push off and spin around the marker with the ball.

The Scottish international and Liverpool forward, Dalglish, was particularly skillful at backing into markers to 'fix' them and use them to push off for a quick turn and an even quicker shot at goal.

Very tight marking against a dangerous attacker makes team mates reluctant to pass to him, which is what it is intended to do. Clever passers in soccer learn that passes aimed at a marked player's feet but played down a line to one side of him allows him a chance of turning 'off' his marker. In these situations, the back must hold position inside the attacker so that his movement when turning keeps his body between the attacker and the goal.

The positional struggle means that each player tries to run the other off the ball. For defenders there must be only one winner. Any weakness when struggling for position while both are turning towards goal gives the attacker an advantage and the back may find himself literally 'on the outside looking in'.

During Italy's 'top of the world' period in the eighties, Claudio Gentile of Juventus, together with club and country team mate, Marco Tardelli, were among the best tight markers I have ever seen. Touch tight or shirt tight, it was all the same to them. At times Gentile seemed so tight as to directly interfere with his opponent's breathing.

## 6.14  Split Vision.

Where possible, most markers prefers to see their immediate opponent and what is happening to the ball at the same time or with as little positional adjustment as possible. Overmuch attention to the ball (ball watching) allows clever attackers to ghost out of sight and out of contact. Over concentration on marking means that the marker and his opponent are often isolated from the game while  conducting a personal 1 v 1 struggle. At times this is justified but it means that the marker cannot be expected to contribute much to an integrated defensive organization.

Clearly all that has been said about marking priorities also has important implications for attackers. They must work equally hard in learning skills which help them to do everything a defender tries to stop them doing.

## 6.2.  Tracking.

When he isn't marking an opponent, a defender almost certainly will be tracking one or even two.

Tracking means watching and following, to a limited extent, an opponent's movements from a distance. That distance is never so great as to prevent the defender from moving from a tracking role to tight marking as quickly as necessary. If one defender can't he must be able to direct another defender to do so. . . quickly.

Good tracking skill enables a defender to remain part of a team's total defensive structure while exerting a kind of remote control over an opponent. The opponent's movements will affect the defender's position but will not control it. In fact, a very skillful defender can track one opponent while marking another even while half covering a co-defender. This is known as 'splitting' opponents.

## 6.3 Closing down.

Tight marking serves different purposes according to the state of play in a game which in turn affects the tactical requirements of players. If not in a tight marking position already, the first requirement of a defender is to know how to move into one. This is the 'closing down' skill referred to. Full backs must develop these techniques because they are frequently involved in moving from deep, covering positions behind other defenders 'onto' an attacker to whom the ball is likely to be played.

To close down on an opponent effectively, a defender needs to be able to watch all the nearby attackers, including the attacker he expects to have to mark, without them being aware of it. The defender 'scans' them all because the ball may be transferred rapidly between two or even three players each of which may have a different idea of what to do next. Similarly when watching the ball passer a back must judge when that player is giving the ball all his attention before actually striking it. That is the time during which the defender can move from covering one area to a tight containing position in another.

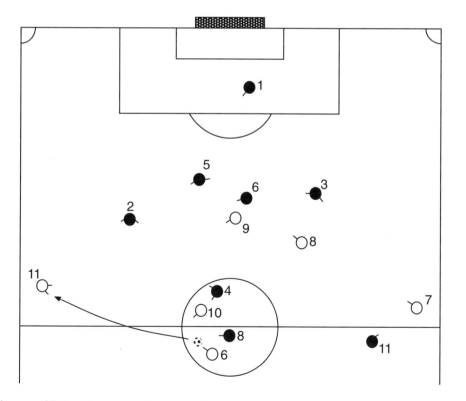

**Diagram 37**. Inviting a pass to opponents.

## 6.4 Inviting a pass.

A full-back who has been unsuccessful in trying to read the intentions of interpassing opponents may decide that the best solution is to simplify their action options for them by offering them a target for their passes. The target player on offer must be outside the defensive structure. In diagram 37, the right back, black 2, has deliberately refrained from closing down on his wing opponent as opposing build up play moves in his direction. He is offering the attacking team an obvious pass possibility. He does so while preparing to close down on that attacker very quickly should his offer be accepted. A wide back will then try to isolate that opponent with the ball and 'box' him in using the sideline to help him.

All defenders should develop the deception skill of being ready without showing it. The adoption of a crouching position or any physical position of athletic readiness to move quickly will alert opponents and deter them from passing. A relaxed air of casual disinterest will be the best attitude to adopt. Beware of opponents who look bored or fed up: in high class soccer they are the players often most acutely aware of what is going on.

The move to close down into an intercepting, tackling or containing position begins when the full-back is sure that the pass is 'on'. He can only judge this from the knowledge that most players need to drop their eyes to the ball at the very last split second before hitting it, to make sure that their contact is perfect. That is the time when the full-back makes his move and it should be a smooth acceleration into action rather than violent and sudden. Nothing should be done to trigger off the passing player's awareness of possible interference.

Knowledge of these deceptive skills isn't the special preserve of defenders of course. When this book becomes available to all, everyone will know what everyone else is thinking!

Effective closing down is not possible unless the defender judges his approach speed correctly: too much, too far and he will have to brake too late to hold a balanced containing position, to make a clean interception or to tackle. When closing down it is easier to speed up over the last few yards than to slow down.

## 6.5 Covering.

Having lost the ball, a team. . . all of it. . . must take up the individual, group and team deployments which, together, are basic to defensive strategy. If these positional commitments are to work, the players. . . all of them. . . must understand the relationship between each part.

Defensive strategies set out what a team is trying to achieve when defending and how, collectively, they will go about it. Without an agreed strategy, players are left to sort out individual problems as and when they occur. Where this is so, if one defender is defeated, the defensive group of which he is a part is unlikely to know what to do to remedy matters. Defensive chaos results when little if any consideration is given to the effect which defeat in one area will have on defending in others.

Generally speaking, when opponents have the ball in their own half of the pitch,

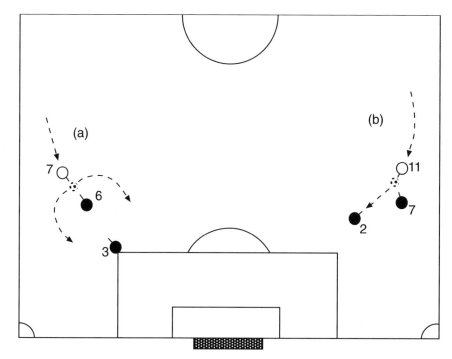

Diagram 38 (a) and (b).

opponents nearest to the ball become in effect first defenders who try to contain, or delay, opposing attacking play and deflect it into pre-determined parts of the pitch. Delay buys time for a second rank of defenders to pick up and mark advancing opponents. All this maximizes difficulty for those opponents to build up and develop play through mid-field. Control of mid-field allows defending backs to mark opposing strikers tightly, to cover potentially dangerous areas and to balance the defense. How these three aims are achieved is a matter for group and individual tactical skills.

An effective covering position enables a defender to deal with (contain) an opponent should that opponent break free of and past another defender. When an attacker does break free he is likely to be under stress from the effort involved; that is when a covering player should be moving in to challenge.

A covering position is determined by the angle at which the covering player positions himself behind the first defender, the distance he is behind him and the speed with which he can move from a covering into a challenging position.

In diagram 38 (a), the full-back, black 3, is at too fine an angle behind the first defender who is facing the ball and too far away from him. If attacker white 7 dribbles past on either side of the first defender, the covering player offers no real barrier.

In diagram 38 (b), defender, black 7, is showing his opponent, white 11, an inside option and the covering player, black 2, has widened his covering angle and short-

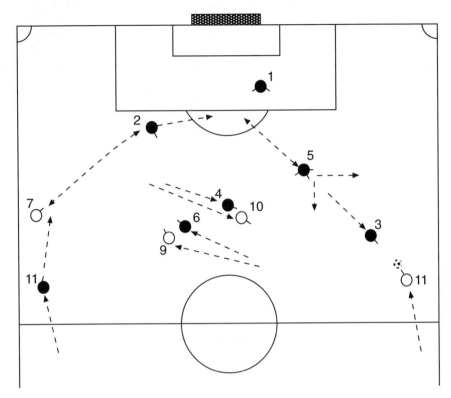

**Diagram 39.** Cover and balance among the backs.

ened his covering distance accordingly. The attacker with the ball will be aware of the threat which the covering player poses and the probability of immediate challenge if he beats the first defender. In a sound covering position, the covering player will make the attacker have second thoughts about attempting to dribble.

Making opponents change their minds is an important defensive skill. Forced to change his mind frequently, an attacker may become confused: if he doesn't know what to do, for sure his team mates won't.

Confusing attackers is the first step towards dislocating their attacking tactics. A wide full-back. . . a good one that is. . . makes many alterations to his position during play, most of which may not bring him into contact with the ball. Their purpose is to disturb the judgment of opponents some distance away: in other words to confuse them.

## 6.51 Dropping Off to Cover and Balance Defense.
As the opposing attack moves over the half way line, and the point of attacking threat switches from side to side, a defender will close down on or drop off from an opponent as play is transferred in his direction or away from it.

In diagram 39, the full-back's line of travel to mark and cover is shown. The

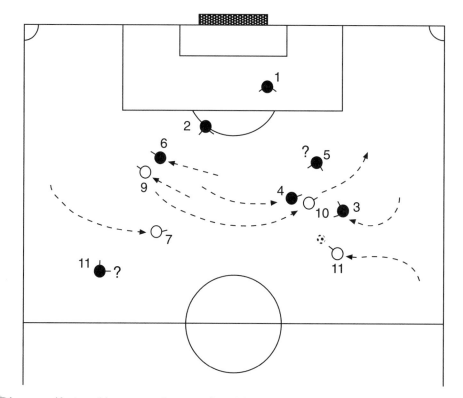

**Diagram 40.** Attacking moves into usual positions.

sweeper may move across and behind the back line to give some cover near to the ball. The far side full-back, black 2 in this case, balances the whole back line and controls space behind the sweeper. The wider the attacking threat is, the more impor- ance he will give to his covering responsibilities. However, it is dangerous to be categorical about positioning, especially on paper.

Full central cover may require a far side back to relax his marking grip on a dangerous opponent. If, to cover centrally, he has to relax his grip on a particularly dangerous opponent, white 7 say, the nearest player to that opponent, in this case black 11, may have to become an auxiliary marking back. That is why all players should receive coaching in the duties and skills of all the positions which they could be expected to fill from time to time.

Very quick backs might reduce the extent of their far side central cover to be a few yards closer to a dangerous player. Taking calculated risks and making correct decisions is what good defending is all about. The back reduces his covering angle and distance to be in a better position to move out and close down on the dangerous opponent quickly. Other defenders having been told what is happening adjust their own positions accordingly.

An intelligent, dangerous attacker may move deliberately in the opposite direction to the full-back towards mid-field or even across the field, diagram 40. He does so first, to worry the full-back: second, to tempt the full-back to move away from his chosen covering position: third, to move into a position that much closer to the action in order to offer himself as an easier target for passes.

In these circumstances, the full-back must have a well organized tactical under-
standing with one of his own mid-field or forward players. As the dangerous opponent moves away from the full-back, another player is nominated to track or mark him. Ideally, the far side full-back's covering distance and angle should enable him to move into the central defensive area or move out to close down on any wide attacker as the ball is in flight to one or the other. Any tendency to exaggerate one position will cause the other position to be more exposed.

In the twin centre back system, covering and marking positions are placed under so much greater strain especially by central attackers who are clever at keeping the two central backs as far from each other as possible.

In diagram 41, the two central backs, blacks 4 and 5, can move forward onto or drop back off each of the central forwards as circumstances demand. This is partic-ularly so where the two wide backs are willing to swing into full covering positions centrally and forego the need to move out to tackle or block wide attackers. When central attackers take up positions much further apart, central cover is much more difficult, sometimes impossible, hence the invention of the sweeper.

Attackers may try to develop play initially in wide positions, then move centrally before reversing play behind the wide backs. Covering assistance from central defense is impossible in these circumstances. That has been a major tactical weak-ness in English defensive organization, from the national team down, for three decades.

A sweeper deployed behind the backs can cover spaces between them and he can move to threaten any reversal of attacking play behind one of the wide backs know-ing that the far side full-back can cover centrally, diagram 42. These are forms of what used to be known as sliding back play.

Any soccer team worth the name, trying to succeed in high grade soccer without an extra back, simply won't! And a picket player may only partially solve the prob-lem. As one centre back drops off to act, temporarily, as a sweeper, the picket player drops back to replace him.

The timing of different moves to mark or cover must be practiced to perfection. Attackers are hardly likely to hang about for the convenience of defenders involved in positional changes. . at least mine wouldn't.

## 6.6 Recovering.

Inevitably, backs make challenges. . . tackles or interceptions. . . which fail. An opponent with the ball will escape towards goal or the goal line or towards the next defender. The attacker may seek to draw that defender out of a covering position so that exploitable space and at least one free attacker can be created in a more central position.

Full backs must know their defensive priorities. They are worth reviewing.

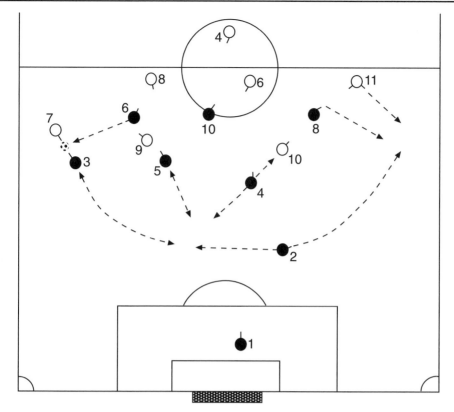

**Diagram 41**. Wide back cover for twin central marking backs.

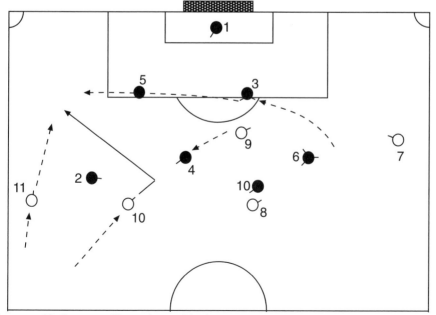

**Diagram 42.** Sweeper (5) moving to black a reverse pass move and covered by the 'far side' back. Black 6.

(a) Defenders must prevent direct shots at goal.

(b) Anyone free and in position to shoot, should the ball arrive, must be challenged urgently.

(c) Defenders must cover any other defender who, if beaten by an attacker with the ball, could shoot.

(d) Defenders must keep the ball away from shooting areas.

From these defensive 'commandments', a beaten full-back's priorities when recovering are clear.

(a) He must recover into a position between the goal and the player with the ball, as quickly as possible.

(b) Having recovered to a 'goal-side' position, he must quickly locate the area of defensive weakness brought about by his original defeat. This is likely to be away from the immediate action and to the far side of the area in front of the goal. Other defenders will have moved across to contain their opponents' break through and defense will be weakest where a defender furthest from the action has moved into a central position.

Occasionally, for tactical reasons, recovery may be down the shortest line towards the attacker with the ball. This attacker may be known to want to run the ball at and past opponents in the last quarter of the pitch and to shoot. He may be capable of defeating one, two or three opponents on the way.

Maradonna, the Argentinian attacker, and the incomparable Péle of Brazil were always seeking to make high speed, dribbling runs at goal. And they shot effectively more often then not. A recovering defender prepared to harass such players from the back with a facing defender refusing to tackle and working hard to contain them from the front causes even great players serious problems. Squeezed from the back and the front, an attacker is likely to evade the pressure by moving sideways and that represents success to the defenders. Anything is better than allowing an attacker to run at goal, especially when he is close to the sanctuary of the penalty area. Opponents' penalty areas are sanctuaries for fast, close dribbling attackers; they are relatively safe inside a penalty area.

The further away from goal a defeated defender is, the more he might recover down a direct line to the attacker who beat him. This depends upon the team's defending strategy. If that strategy requires all the forwards to sustain high pressure attempts to regain possession, the beaten defender chasing his opponent with the ball will seek a position where he can add to defensive pressure around the ball or even make a positive challenge for it.

Generally speaking, however, recovering defenders seek secondary defending positions behind a team mate who is committed to containing the opponent with the ball. The only circumstance in which a recovering defender might become the first

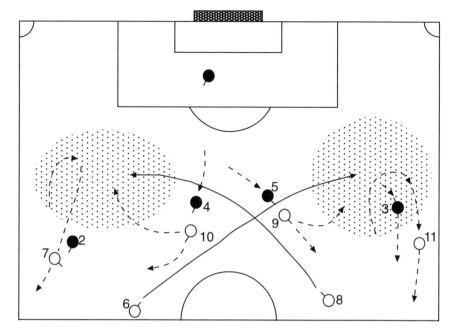

**Diagram 43**. Creating attacking space by tempting backs out of it.

defender would be if the attacker with the ball turned back towards him or moved sideways. Even then, the recovering player's challenge might be more threatening than real. A secure defending position has a higher priority than merely chasing an attacker with the ball.

Defending with pools of players, two, three or occasionally four strong became an important part of Holland's defensive strategy some years ago. The nearer to their opponents' goal when they lost the ball, the greater the commitment of nearby Dutch players to early, high pressure attempts to regain possession or at worst to worry opponents on or near to the ball. Players used their considerable speed and often full-stretch, sliding tackles to try to regain possession. Even Johann Cruyff, world-class master craftsman of attacking play, not normally conspicuous for defensive industry, joined in this high pressured containment strategy. When opponents established controlled possession of the ball and began to move it towards the Dutch half of the field, then The Dutch 'guerrillas' recovered at more leisured pace into the basic team defensive structure normally set up just over the half way line.

## 6.7  Denying space.

Occasionally, opponents' attacking tactics demand unorthodox defensive counters. This is particularly true where opponents' tactics aim to create and exploit attacking space behind or within the back defensive curtain.

An attacking team may try to create the optimum space behind the wide backs, for example.

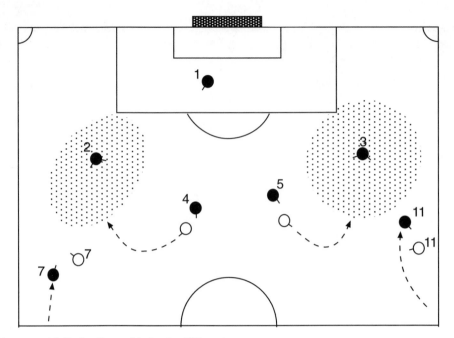

**Diagram 44.** Defending wide backs filling deep space.

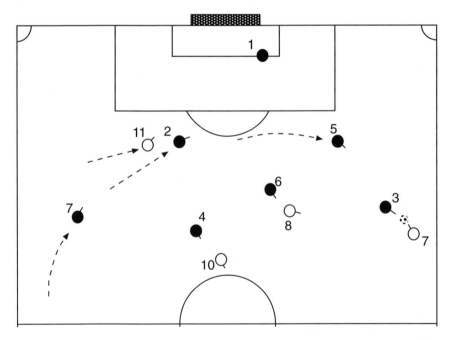

**Diagram 45.** An attacker behind but close to the far side back and able to judge offside to perfection.

In diagram 43, two wide attackers have been sent forward to draw the wide backs. The attackers have pushed forward to play like old fashioned wingers. Having attracted the backs' attention, the attackers gradually move back towards their own mid-field to draw the backs with them. Their intention is to create large unoccupied areas behind the wide backs. The two central attackers similarly draw the attention of the two centre backs to hold them in central positions. The attacking team's strategy may be to play passes into the wide areas for the two central attackers to run for late and quickly.

These wide runs are intended to stretch the back defense while ensuring possession by an attacker close to the penalty area or even occasionally within it. An attacker who can turn with the ball in these areas can cause considerable problems. To counter this strategy of building up in the 'wide channels', as they are called, the defending team may pull back mid-field players or attackers to mark the opposing wide players, thereby leaving the backs free to occupy the target space, diagram 44.

There's no gain from playing the ball into space which is already occupied by a defender; but it happens, particularly among severely 'programmed' teams which play the game by numbers.

Where a defending team's far-side back is expected to pivot towards a central covering position, he may be disconcerted if an attacker moves over with him, keeping in an on-side position almost as near to goal as the back but behind him. An attacker in this position is particularly dangerous because he, of all the players, is in the best possible position to judge the 'off-side, on-side' situation, diagram 45.

If the back marks him and moves over with him, he must be conscious of the over balancing effect this move will have. A very large area has been created between his now central defending position and the far side touch-line. In these circumstances, it may pay the defending team to withdraw a mid-field or a forward player, black 7 say, to occupy that space and deter opponents from trying to use it.

Filling space to prevent its use during the build up of attacking play is occasionally necessary. However, backs who always seek to fill space rather than mark opponents need to be watched. Filling space when 'one to one' close marking is the real need is a soft option and dangerous. If one or two. . . or more. . . backs are always looking to fill space, then one, two or more opponents somewhere else on the pitch are unmarked, free to set impossible problems for other defenders by outnumbering them.

An aging full-back will enjoy directing the energy of willing young players in front of him; players keen to do all the running and tackling while he fills space and takes the credit for intercepting misplaced passes induced by their hard work; I remember it well. Advancing age and hard work don't go well together.

## 6.8 Containing.

The four defensive 'commandments' set out earlier are entirely complementary. If a defending team is wholly successful at preventing opponents from having one direct shot at goal that team cannot score. The more that the defending team can prevent the ball from being moved into areas close to the goal, the less the likelihood of shots occurring. . or, for that matter, of 'own goals' being scored.

Resisting opposing play so that it never penetrates the key shooting or the key delivery areas is called containing. It is a vital aspect of defensive play.

When opponents attack, they need certain conditions to help them. First, the player 'on' the ball needs room. . . personal space. . . and time to judge and then use forward passing or forward dribbling options. Good players make those judgments long before they actually receive the ball; they are always making and changing judgments about what to do IF the ball comes; whether it comes or not is immaterial. Poor players only decide what to do after the ball has arrived. That makes them so much easier to 'read' and contain.

### 6.81  Closing down and blocking.

The first requirement of a containing defender must be to deny an opponent with the ball the space. . and the time. . to turn with the ball, to shoot, to pass it forward or to begin to dribble.

The nearer the defender is to his opponent, the more that opponent is aware of his presence. Intimidated, many attackers move or pass sideways or backwards rather than run the risk of confronting, colliding with or hitting the defender with a pass.

The nearer the defender, the more the player 'on' the ball must concentrate on keeping it. Of course outstanding players do not need to look at the ball to control it: at least not much. In fact they may give a false impression of insecurity on the ball to tempt a defender to have a go for it.

Defenders must be alert to the confidence trickery of exceptional players: fortunately there are few of us left!

It follows that where an attacker is able to choose to pass or dribble the ball sideways or backwards, he has been allowed too many options and containment has been only partially successful.

### 6.82  Jockeying.

A containing defender must 'jockey' the attacker so that his options are limited, preferably to one. Other defenders must know what the jockeying defender's intentions are and that's a matter for detailed coaching in realistic practice situations and for good 'in the game' communication.

Few, if any, coaches in my experience bother to teach inter-player or even coach-player communication. There is a skill involved; it can be taught: it should be!

Jockeying done well enables other defenders to attempt pass interceptions safely and to take up tight challenging and containing positions themselves. Wide backs, faced with dangerous wide attackers may jockey them 'inside' forcing them to move and pass across the front of the defense. Central backs may jockey dangerous central strikers towards wide positions and away from profitable shooting areas.

## 6.83 Retreating.

Jockeying by full-backs may involve closing an opponent down quickly, holding a close position, refusing temptations to challenge, even running away from him (retreating). A wide back, faced with a direct and decisive opponent may' show him the 'line' and hope to confine or trap him in the narrow channel formed by the side-line and the back's line of retreat. Retreating gives the jockeying player a yard or two start should the opponent try to use surprise or superior speed. Players running with the ball, when faced by an opponent moving away from them, tend to slow down. The jockeying player, often, can bring even the fastest of opponents almost to a halt by retreating at a varying pace.

A centre back, on the other hand cannot really afford to show an opponent any sort of direction because in central defensive areas one stride may be all that an attacker needs to release a shot. A central back will close down on his opponent so that the opponent hasn't the time or the space to pull back his leg for a shot at goal. He may, if he knows his opponent well enough, jockey the attacker onto his weaker foot. He must be sure of the weakness and even so he must block or threaten to block any attempt to shoot. Even the most one footed player may try his 'swinger', his useless foot, and get a successful contact.

In the 1966 World Cup final, Geoff Hurst, the England forward, hit the ball with his swinger, his left foot. By his own admission his intention was to kill time by launching the ball into outer orbit.

The intended launch went wrong and he scored with searing power.

Central backs must be very skillful. . . and patient. . . in shepherding attackers away from goal. Hence the importance for backs (and all other defenders) to deny opponents space in which to turn with the ball towards goal. Whichever form it takes, jockeying must guide the attacking player in the direction chosen by the jockeying defender and in a direction which will be the most advantageous to his team.

It is crucially important that the jockeying defender doesn't tackle for possession until he is absolutely certain that he can win the ball or knock it out of play. Jockeying an opponent into a 'dead area' causes him to move with the ball into a part of the field from which there is simply no-where else to go.

On the other hand a player being jockeyed to keep the ball 'alive' is controlled so that he must pass to a team mate who cannot receive the ball safely or so that he him-self is caught in possession. Either way, the team seeking to gain possession is enabled to counter attack.

## 6.84 Working an opponent.

Most frequently, jockeying involves a patient refusal by a back to be drawn into a tackle unless he is two hundred percent certain of winning it. The jockeying player 'out waits to out-wit' his opponent and forces him to make the first move. For different tactical reasons, it may be necessary for a back to work hard to compel his opponent to make the first move. He may do this by faking moves to tackle, faking moves in this direction or that, pretending to move too close to his opponent. All these moves are intended to put the opponent under stress and thereby not able to retain his composure on the ball or his balance.

An attacker who is himself very patient and very successful at pulling or flicking the ball away from tackles at the last split second, depends upon defenders losing their composure and striking for the ball. England's Stanley Matthews, one of the greatest dribbling wingers of all time, had infinite patience. Matthews didn't merely wait for an opponent to tackle, he made countless moves faking to play the ball with the inside and outside of his right foot to tempt opponents into the tackle. His flickering right foot, moving the ball fractionally one way and then the other, had a hypnotizing effect on opposing backs. Only backs with as much patience as Matthews himself remained unbeaten. In fact, as all outstanding players do, he turned the tables on most defenders by using their own methods against them. And while he was setting them up to draw them into losing tackles for possession, he moved towards them so that they were backing away. . . thinking they were jockeying him effectively. In reality, he was jockeying them away from the touch-line entrapment channel to ensure that he had enough space to move in any direction but more often than not outside his opponent.

## 6.85 Inviting a Pass.

We have seen how it is possible for a defender to control an opponent with the ball by presenting him with limited options and maneuvering him into positions from which he only has one choice and that a poor one.

Attackers. . . skillful attackers that is. . . seek to play passes into space behind their opponents and especially behind full-backs. These can lead to direct running shots at goal or dangerous crosses but above all they make defenders play facing their own goal. The outlawed pass back into the goalkeeper's hands requires modern backs to be more skillful in turning with he ball and in interpassing with other backs.

Rather than allow the ball to be played behind him, a clever back will deliberately relax his marking position on an attacker and 'offer' that attacker as a target for a pass, diagram 46. Where an attacker with the ball is free and able to choose when and to whom he will pass, it is better to offer him a pass to a forward player who can be marked quickly after the ball has arrived, than to mark the forward so tightly that a pass can be played behind the marking player, black 3 in diagram 46.

Where a team plays with a sweeper, the central markers may offer the opponent 'on' the ball an option to pass to the feet of central strikers facing him. This enables the markers to make direct challenges, even interceptions, rather than to contain play. They know that they are reasonably secure should they slip while trying for an interception or while tackling.

## 6.9 Intercepting Passes.

## 6.91 Anticipation.

The skill of intercepting is based upon the back's ability to:
- judge (read) the probability of a pass to a certain player.

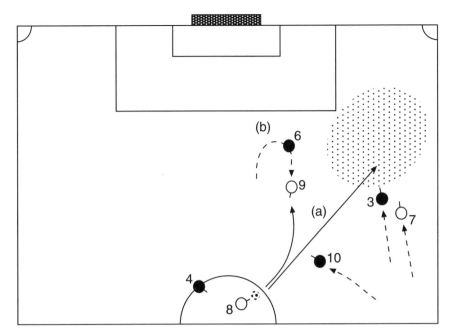

**Diagram 46.** A back, black 6, offers an easy target for a pass. To discourage a more dangerous option (a).

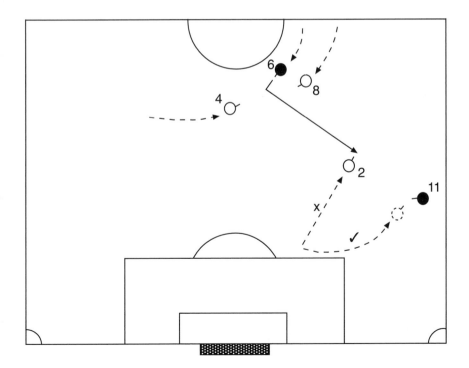

**Diagram 47.** Intercepting too far inside the target player.

- estimate the pass's traveling time against the intercepting player's speed in moving to an intercepting position.

- take into account the movement of the target player away from the potential interceptor, perhaps towards the passer.

If it sounds complicated, it is! The precise answers to these and other questions have to be computed instantly almost. And to complicate matters further, an intercepting back must be aware that all the information upon which his assessments are based could be false.

## 6.92  Deception.

Deceptively skillful opponents will deliberately send out action 'clues' to mislead a defender and draw him away from goal (and other defenders) perhaps tempting him into an interception so that passes may be switched to other attackers moving into the space behind him.

A mistake frequently made by wide backs moving out to intercept is to do so down a line too far inside the target player, diagram 47. If it comes off, interception leaves the intercepting defender in possession of the ball and moving, probably, into free space. If it doesn't come off. . . the wind may move the ball on a fraction quicker or the interceptor may find his move for the ball is hampered by poor ground conditions. . . then the defender himself is out of the play and stranded. Interceptions should be made down a line as close to the target player as possible. If something goes wrong with the interception, the defender is only marginally worse placed than his opponent. Psychologically, there is nothing worse for a pass receiver to be comfortably setting himself to accept a pass only to find the ball whipped off his toes at the last moment. The shock and the surprise of late interceptions cause attackers minds to be temporarily 'blown'. The experience makes them apprehensive when calling for and receiving passes which may be switched from one side of the field to the other. They try to move further away from possible interceptors which means away from the danger areas.

Acting plays a great part in high class soccer as it does at the top level in all games. And, like good acting anywhere, it must be absolutely convincing. Exceptional soccer players go to enormous lengths to hide their real intentions.

A full-back intent upon intercepting very late and at speed must never be caught preparing himself for that action. He may think that he needs a crouch start or to edge towards the target player in order to get there in time but if he is caught preparing to do it, he kills the possibility of an interception.

A clever back will put on an air of casual, even bored disinterest. He may create the false impression that he is a 'ball watcher' and not an opponent watcher. He may deliberately move away from his intended line of attack before moving down it. He may even act as if he is more concerned with his surgical underwear or his hair style than with what opponents are doing.

There are a lot of potential Oscar winners outside Hollywood: most of them are in soccer!

## 6.93 Body Blocking.

The action of interception isn't merely a matter of sticking a leg out and in front of an opponent at the right time. Skillful attackers may draw an opponent into an inter- ception and, as the back moves to reach in front of his opponent for the ball, the attacker moves his body fractionally across the same line. Either the defender tries to avoid contact and makes the interception difficult or impossible to complete or the two players collide. Because the attacker has deliberately set up the body block, it is almost certain that he will knock the defender out of the play.

When making interceptions backs and other defenders must assume an opponent's intention to use the body block and set his body to resist it. He must drop his near side shoulder as low as he can without fouling his opponent. Shoulder charges are legitimate when made shoulder to shoulder but it is not easy for referees to judge these actions precisely. If the block seems reasonably fair it will be allowed but backs must remember that referees see two sides in any action. The interceptor has most to lose if he attacks the ball loosely, casually or too soon. Better for a back to knock down his opponent when trying for an interception than to be knocked down himself. His judgment must be based upon two considerations; the danger created if the challenge is weak and the danger to another player if the block is violent.

Violence is an excessive use of force in player to player confrontations. Physical contact between players is a part of soccer but dangerous play, intimidation and violence. . . which are often the same things. . . are not.

## 6.94 Shot and Pass Blocking.

The backs must prevent shots at goal and passes towards players who might be able to shoot. Wide positions, in the channels formed by the edges of the penalty area and the touch lines are those most favored for cross-field passes (crosses) towards the dangerous shooting areas. These crosses must be blocked if possible. It is even more important that, should the pass arrive and an opponent get in a shot at goal, the ball must be blocked as soon as or even before it leaves the attacker's foot.

To block a cross, a wide back  moves or recovers to a position inside, level with and perhaps a yard away from the opponent who is about to cross the ball. As the attacker pushes the ball forward to take a long stride into his kicking action, the back accelerates, changing his stride if necessary, so that his blocking leg, the leg furthest from his opponent, is in stride with his opponent's outside (kicking) leg. Fractionally before the kicker's foot strikes the ball, the back will stretch out his blocking leg, furthest from the ball, so that his foot is not much more than two feet from the ball as it is kicked; it may be closer. The further away the blocking foot is as the ball is kicked, the firmer the ankle and foot must be to block the kick cleanly and safely.

The nearer to the ball the blocking foot is at impact, the safer the block. Central backs may have to block from the front, i.e. 'face on', when direct shots are attempted. The back watches for the attacker setting himself for the swing of his shooting leg. As soon as he feels that the attacker is committed to a shot, the back stretches his leg forward so that the sole and cleats of his blocking foot are as close to the ball as possible. Inexperienced players may feel that if they mistime the block, the ball will hit them painfully in the face. They stretch into the blocking position remotely and half-heartedly. In fact the nearer to the ball the blocking foot is when the ball is kicked, the less likely it is for the ball to fly past it.

The danger, if any, is to the player shooting. A late challenge means that the ball has gone and the attacker's foot is likely to swing through to contact the cleats of the blocker's boot. The result can be painful and may cause serious injury to the shooting player. When the block is made deliberately late, the guilty player should be sent off and severely punished.

All tackles and similar attempts to play the ball, between two players, depend for their safety on the intentions of both players to do so fairly and with due regard to each other's safety. Recklessness must be dealt with severely; recklessness and violent play are the enemies of skill and soccer, above all else, must be a game of skill.

## 6.95 Cutting the Lines of Passes.

Occasionally a full-back will be caught out of position and unable to prevent an opponent from delivering a pass and even less able to prevent the target player from receiving it. In diagram 48, the full-back, black 2, has been supporting advanced attacking play but the attack has broken down. An opponent, white 8, is preparing to pass to white 11. The full-back cannot make a challenge to stop the pass deliverer and he is unlikely to recover into containing position against the intended pass receiver. As he turns to funnel back along the shortest line towards goal and a reasonable defensive position, he angles his run across what he anticipates may be white 8's line of pass.

By cutting across the player's passing line he may make that player check his pass, giving the full-back and other defenders an extra few seconds in which to recover. Alternatively he may be lucky enough to intercept it.

In diagram 49, the picket player, black 6, realizing that the central back, black 4, is exposed in a losing one against one situation if white 10 completes his pass, deliberately runs across the probable line of the pass fractionally before it is released. By doing so he hopes to make the opposing player re-think his passing option. Even if the pass is delivered he may have gained the extra seconds, enabling defensive cover to be re-established. As we have seen, reading the passing intentions of opponents is an important skill which backs must learn and which coaches must teach. It is not enough to hope that some may pick up the skill.

During close inter-passing moves, interceptions may appear to have been made almost through 'second sight'. Often they are made because a defender, changing position, happens to cut across an opponent's line of pass just as he is making it. If a back is caught out of position. . . and it happens, even to the best of us. . . he might as well make himself a nuisance by making his recovery run and threatening the possible lines of opponents' passes at the same time.

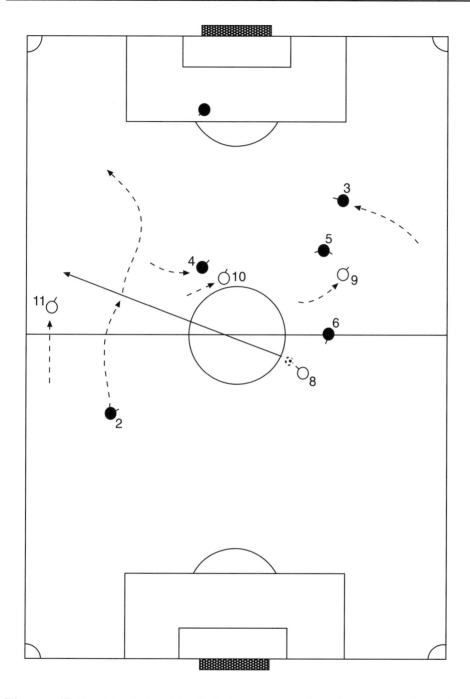

**Diagram 48.** Caught out of position defender runs to cut through an opponent's passing line.

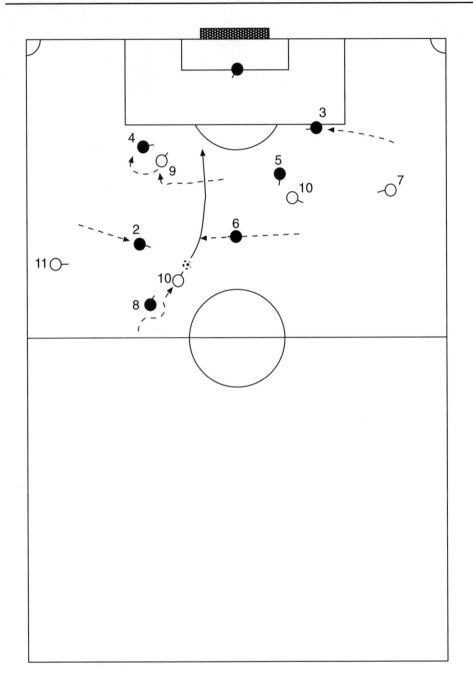

**Diagram 49.** Cutting across and threatening an opponent's line of pass.

# Chapter 7
# Special Technical Considerations.

## 7.1 Short and Medium Inter-Passing Skills.

Accurate passing techniques must be mastered by all players. The backs will often be required to play to feet safely over relatively short distances, ten to thirty yards say and frequently across the pitch. Opponents will be looking for interception opportunities. Cross-field interpassing must be safe and passing angles easily changeable where opponents are prepared to move players forward to pressurize the backs.

I never say never but one touch passing exchanges are not really for backs: two touch most certainly are. One touch passing may be worth the risk when it occurs deep in the opponents' half and when attacking skills are most valuable. The state of play in a particular game may warrant extra quick transference of the ball from one area or one player to another, thereby justifying the employment of urgent techniques.

Accurate, two touch interpassing sequences tend to 'kill off' opponents' enthusiasm for sustained, running challenges because they enable backs to transfer the ball to different areas of the pitch swiftly and surely. One touch passing sequences among backs in their own half run the risk of misplacement or of over weighting; the risks are too great.

Inter-passing among the backs must always be for the convenience of the receiver: aimed preferably at the foot furthest away from any conceivable challenger. And that's a point worth noting for coaches preparing interpassing practice. Accuracy in passing is not judged by the ability of one player merely to pass to another. Accuracy in serious soccer is judged by the accuracy of passing to a receiving player's preferred foot. It's not much use, even dangerous, to pass to a player' right foot when he's left footed or when circumstances demand that the ball is kept as far away as possible from a threatening opponent.

## 7.11  Aerial Passing.

In England the trademarks for traditional backs were hard tackling and long kicking up-field. World wide, traditions have changed although I'm not sure that they have in England. . . yet!

Wide backs usually find themselves in possession of the ball with the need to play down narrow. . sometimes extremely narrow. . . channels, to players who may be marked very tightly. An alternative may be to drop the ball into the space behind the wide player. Wide ranging central attackers often use those spaces to draw defenders away from central space. 'Channel passing' involves chipping the ball so that on landing it 'holds up' and doesn't run out of play over the goal line.

Medium length chipping has to be achieved with almost imperceptible changes in preparation body language from, say, a short ground pass down the same line. The same passing techniques are used to feed central attackers moving towards their own backs while closely marked. Passes are chipped to 'die' in front of the receiver or, if that pass might be intercepted, chipped into space behind both players. If the second option is taken, another attacker seeing his team mate marked touch tight must move into the space behind him.

Players seeking to give penetrating passes must always have two action options. Playing to an attacker's feet often involves squeezing a ground pass between two defenders quite close together. The passer may look as if to deliver an aerial pass over them in order to relax their possible awareness of his real intentions.

## 7.12 'Outside In' Passes.

Passes given by a wide back to players in-field must not carry the risk of interception. They need to deceive opponents without surprising the receiver. Usually they will be given when the passer's body language telegraphs a different passing line to deceive opponents but it might also deceive an intended receiver. The passing player will shout the target player's name, but signal a pass in another direction before passing to him. If opponents enjoy first name familiarity with your players then other shouted signals will be needed.

Broadly speaking, when a player decides to give a pass he should always have another option in his mind and that option should be realizable whatever happens. If a player has to change his mind very late, it may pay him to forget any alternative action which he was considering and change his mind again: especially near to his own goal.

Deceptive play by backs is best used infrequently and built on repetitions of safe, orthodox even obvious moves. The more deceptive a player tries to be, the less deceptive he is likely to be.

## 7.13 Swerve Passes.

Playing in narrow channels against opponents working hard to limit his angles of opportunity, a wide back will find it an advantage to be able to hit passes through the air with swerve.

In diagram 50, the centre back, black 5, aims a pass apparently towards a central striker but 'fades' it out towards the wide attacker, black 11.

In diagram 51, the wide back, white 2, hits a cross field pass seemingly away from his target player, white 9, but with late swerve towards him. Faced with swerved passes opponents are never absolutely certain what the purpose or real line of such a pass is.

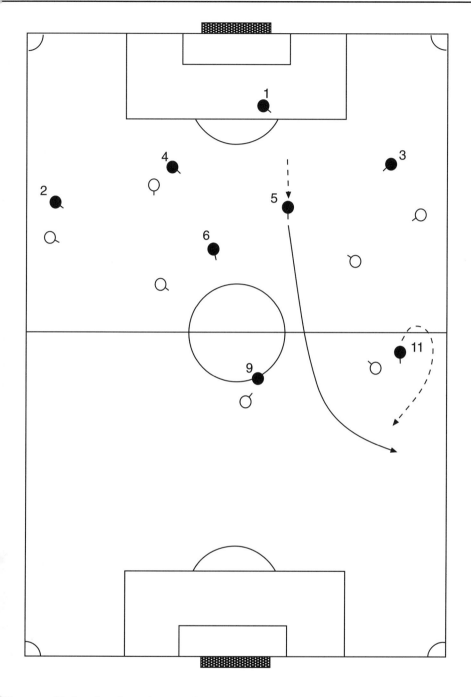

**Diagram 50.** Passing deception. 'Fading' passes away from defenders.

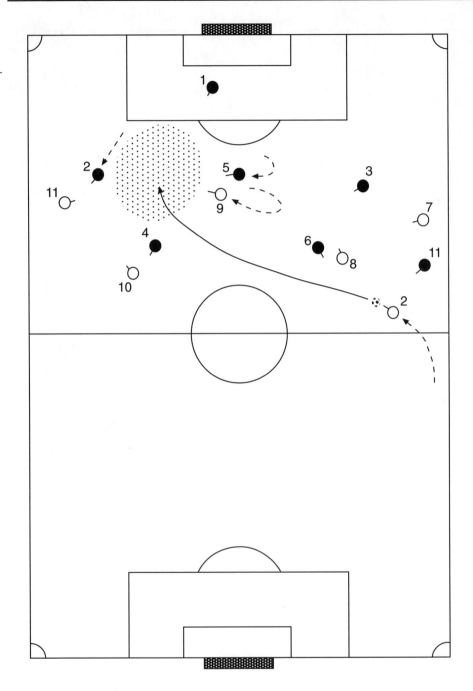

**Diagram 51**. Using swerved passes to deceive opponents.

## 7.14  Changing Passing Angles.

As we have seen, players with the ball need at least two action options in any given situation. A back choosing and 'showing' a passing angle needs to be able to change that angle and pass with no more than two, preferably one further touch. Having controlled the ball and apparently intending to deliver a pass upfield, a skillful player will cut his foot sharply and very late across the ball to find a less obvious target player. His kicking foot swings almost at right angles across his non-kicking, standing foot.

Any controlling touch should allow for either of two totally different passing angles. A controlling move with a player's right foot to his right side produces one sector for his pass. A controlling move to his left side produces a totally different passing sector. And of course different distances and changed angles between the intended kicking foot and the players' receiving position affect the sector over which the ball can be passed.

Understanding how these options can be used to deceive opponents with as little 'give away' as possible is a very important skill for any player irrespective of his playing position.

## 7.15 Deceptive Passing.

### (a) Short Leg Swing.

Deception when passing is improved when a player develops exceptional power from a short leg swing with the minimum back lift of his kicking foot. Normally kicking power is generated by using a long leg swing from the hip, thereby developing foot speed over a long arc. The longer the leg swing the more obvious the direction of the kick and the likely target.

A short leg swing produces deceptive power from the late and very fast extension of the leg at the knee joint. This method of passing has the advantage of allowing for a very late change of passing line  merely by altering the relationship between the kicking foot and the ankle. Additionally this kicking action can be performed on the run and the kick comes from a late and only slight readjustment of a player's normal running stride. For passing effectively through the narrow gaps created by tight defensive deployments this skill is a must.

### (b) Drag.

Deception in ground passing can be achieved by creating a drag effect on the ball. Using the same basic technique as described in (a) the player lowers his contact point on the ball so that the toes are allowed to partially and loosely contact the under surface of the ball. The main force of the kick is still from the instep through the ball's horizontal mid-point but the ball tries to rotate backwards and to resist normal forward rotation. The ball skids during the early part of its travel until forward rotation (roll) takes over. The effect is to make the kick seem much more powerful than it actually is, initially. Opponents tend to assume that the ball is moving too fast to be intercepted but when the ball is past them the drag effect reduces ball speed and makes controlling the ball much easier than seemed possible as the kick was made.

## — 7.2 Making Space.

Safe space for the backs is more often behind them than in front and towards the goalkeeper who, if he is sure in his kicking skills, is the ultimate 'fail safe' outlet. It is important that the backs know how, where and above all when to move to maximize this space.

In diagram 52, the four backs are likely to be pressured by three forward opponents. The crescent formation of the backs demands that the ball is moved swiftly, sometimes hurriedly and very accurately to negate the splitting and closing down intentions of the opponents. Success for the forwards will be to contain the backs and the ball in front of them.To optimize space, the backs must use the whole of the width of the pitch and test the willingness of their opponents to work very hard to pressure them.

In diagram 53, where black 5 has the ball the players on either side of him move forward. Almost certainly those moves will be tracked: if they aren't, those players become passing targets. The player furthest away, black 2, moves back. The ball holder and this free back can interpass with negligible risk. Forward pressing players, in forward or in mid-field positions, do not like to press forward against opponents only to find the ball played behind them.

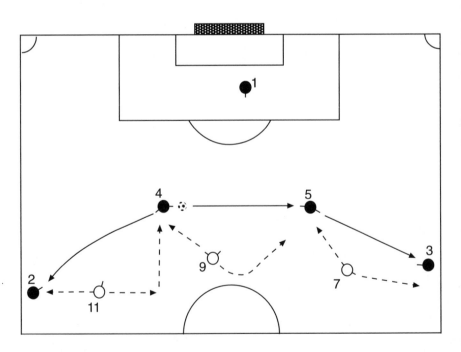

**Diagram 52.** Backs deployed to maximize space under containing pressure.

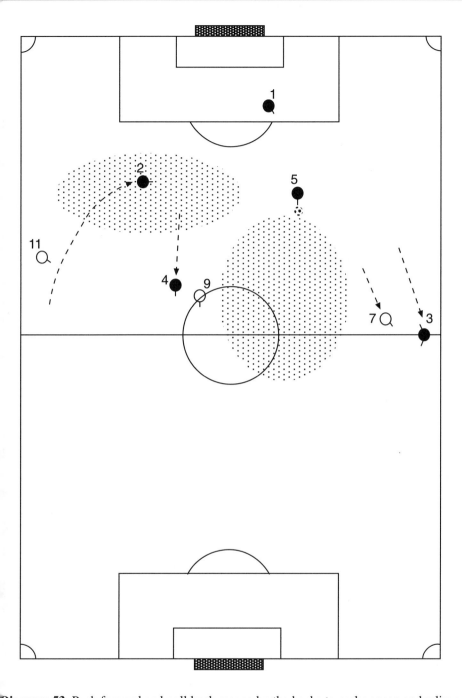

**Diagram 53.** Push forward and pull back moves by the backs to make space and relieve containing pressure.

## 7.3 Holding and Protecting The Ball.

Where a back finds himself isolated in possession of the ball and under pressure from an opponent, he must have the skills to hold onto the ball while shielding it from tackles. This means that he must 'work' the ball with the foot furthest from a challenger and keep his body firmly between that challenger and the ball. This requires not only tight ball working skills but also the physical strength necessary to resist the pushing and pulling which close encounters involve. Challenging players have nothing to lose from making challenges bordering on the illegal since free kicks, not always given, are a small price to pay for occasionally robbing a back of the ball deep in his own half of the pitch.

**Backs, isolated with the ball and near to their own goal, are in 'no win' situations.**

In these circumstances backs cannot readily pass themselves out of trouble, if they try almost certainly they will put team mates into trouble. . . deep into it. Running the ball is the only viable alternative other than kicking the ball out of play.

## 7.4 Controlling Techniques.

In modern soccer possession of the ball is everything almost. Giving the ball away unnecessarily is a crime; at the highest levels it is punished, severely.

Backs are as much responsible for bringing the ball under control and thereby establishing possession as every other player. Kicking possession away for the sake of speed and distance is no longer acceptable back play. Mastery of all controlling skills is important when opponents are looking for the slightest slackness in control to enable them to move in and steal the ball. Not only are defenders required to provide skill and intelligence in attack, attackers are expected to provide tough and predatory defending.

Good defenders develop the ability to hide their actual intentions. When bringing the ball under control, the player's body language indicates every intention to play the ball away first touch. All controlling skills are exact reverses of kicking or heading techniques. The alternative skills should be learned and practiced together at the same time. The majority of coaches teach soccer techniques in isolation and separately.

They are wrong and, worse, they are wasting valuable practice time and learning opportunities. The techniques of soccer, practiced most effectively, are linked together naturally. A player doesn't just trap the ball, he traps the ball to pass or to shoot or to dribble. He doesn't just pass the ball, he has to receive the ball before he can pass it. To dribble effectively, ball control while running at varying speeds cannot be an end in itself. The player dribbles in order to pass or to threaten to pass or to shoot and so on. Soccer techniques must be employed as deceptively as circumstances demand and deception cannot be added later like the icing on a cake.

Deception has to be part of the most basic levels of skill learning. Not only must players hide their real intentions, they must learn to give totally misleading indications as to what those intentions are. When the intention is to control the ball in the air, players must learn to 'shape' as if to give a push volley pass: when about to trap the ball under the sole of the foot, players will look as if they are about to drive the ball upfield. When about to control the ball with the head or the chest, players will ___ move towards the ball as if they are going to head clear powerfully and for distance.

Having given false clues, at the very last moment, the techniques will be reversed so that passes or kicks or headers become controlling skills.

When working alone or with a coach, players must practice the unexpected as part of his or her general skill practice routine. Such is the speed at which the modern game is played and such is the pressure to which all players are subjected by opponents that early, perfect control is a most valuable skill for backs. The ball is frequently in the air. . . in some countries too frequently. . . and the full-backs must be able to 'kill' the ball with that part of the body. . . excluding the hand or arm. . . which will enable them to gain the earliest touch of the ball. Having got to the ball first, control must be instant.

Backs must master all aerial controlling techniques, with head, chest, thigh and with all the various surfaces of the foot, especially the uppermost surface, the instep. A full-back may have to control the ball as it drops steeply in front of or dangerously behind him. Sole of the foot or inside of the foot trapping is very difficult because of the angle of drop and a control failure will spell big trouble. The ball may have to be caught on the instep or on the thigh and lowered gently to the ground in one fluid movement.

The learning and practice situations created by teachers and coaches must be as realistic as possible from stage one. Players must learn to use their imaginations at the earliest possible stages. It is no use practicing techniques in simple situations in which the receiving player is always comfortably facing the ball. The techniques must be taught, learned and practiced in unusual and difficult situations. Creating realistic practice situations while acknowledging the players' immature skills is what soccer teachers and coaches must learn to do. Merely trying to transmit such playing experience as the coach might have will not be enough.

All controlling techniques involve a withdrawal of the intended controlling surface fractionally before impact, thereby absorbing 'ball force' resulting from speed through the air or along the ground. Some coaches refer to the need for a controlling surface to be so relaxed at impact that the surface is effectively knocked back by the ball. Knocked back or withdrawn, the controlling surface must present a soft, non resistant surface to the ball to achieve 'drop dead' control. The controlling player should be as near to the ball's line of flight or movement as possible: preferably immediately behind it.

Modern players should be all round players, capable of playing effectively in all parts of the pitch in all phases of play. Mastery of all the basic skills and the common variations of them should be encouraged at the earliest possible age, certainly nearer to five years of age than to fifteen. Specialist techniques and skills may be acquired later as players realize in which positions, for the most part, they prefer to spend most of their playing time.

# *Other books from* **REEDSWAIN**

Allen Wades NEW Books and others in this series.

PRINCIPLES OF
## Effective
## Coaching
#245 • $14.95

TEACHING THE
## Principles
## of Soccer
#148 • $14.95

POSITIONAL PLAY
## Midfield
#2532: • $12.95

POSITIONAL PLAY
## Strikers
#2533: • $12.95

POSITIONAL PLAY
## Goalkeeping
#2534: • $12.95

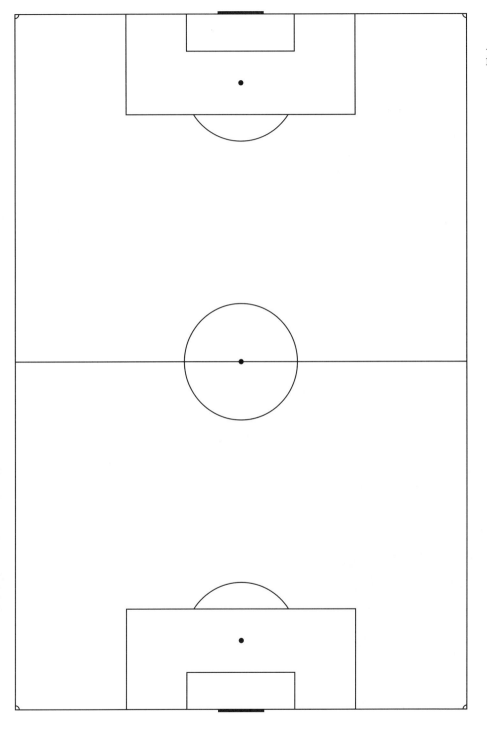

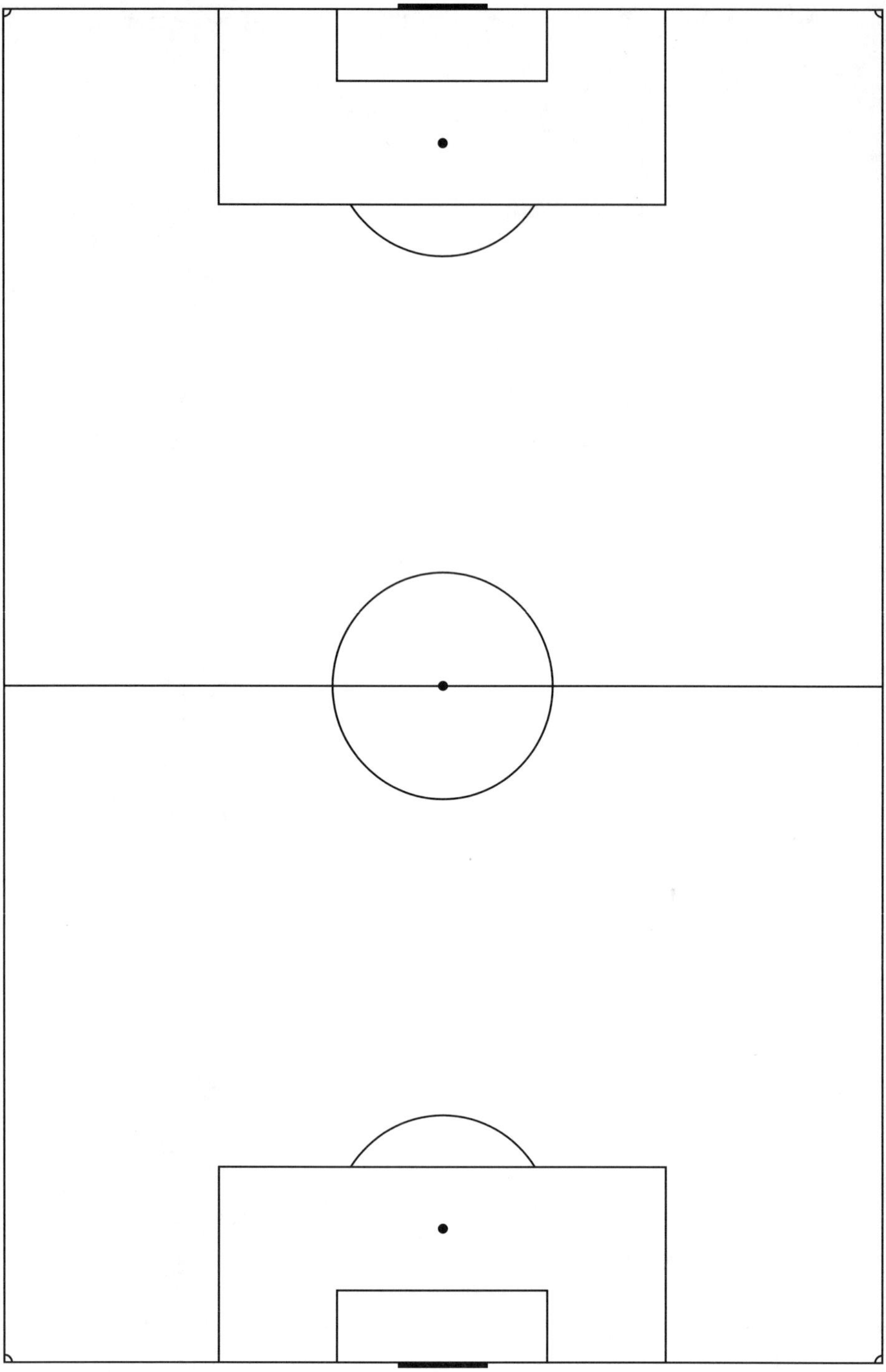

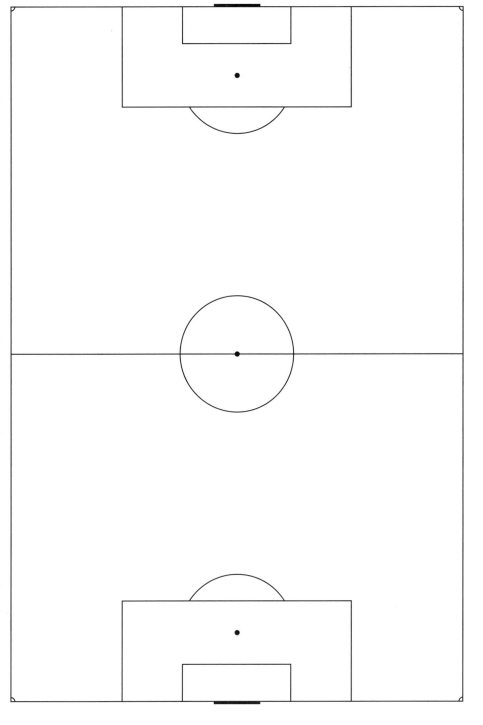

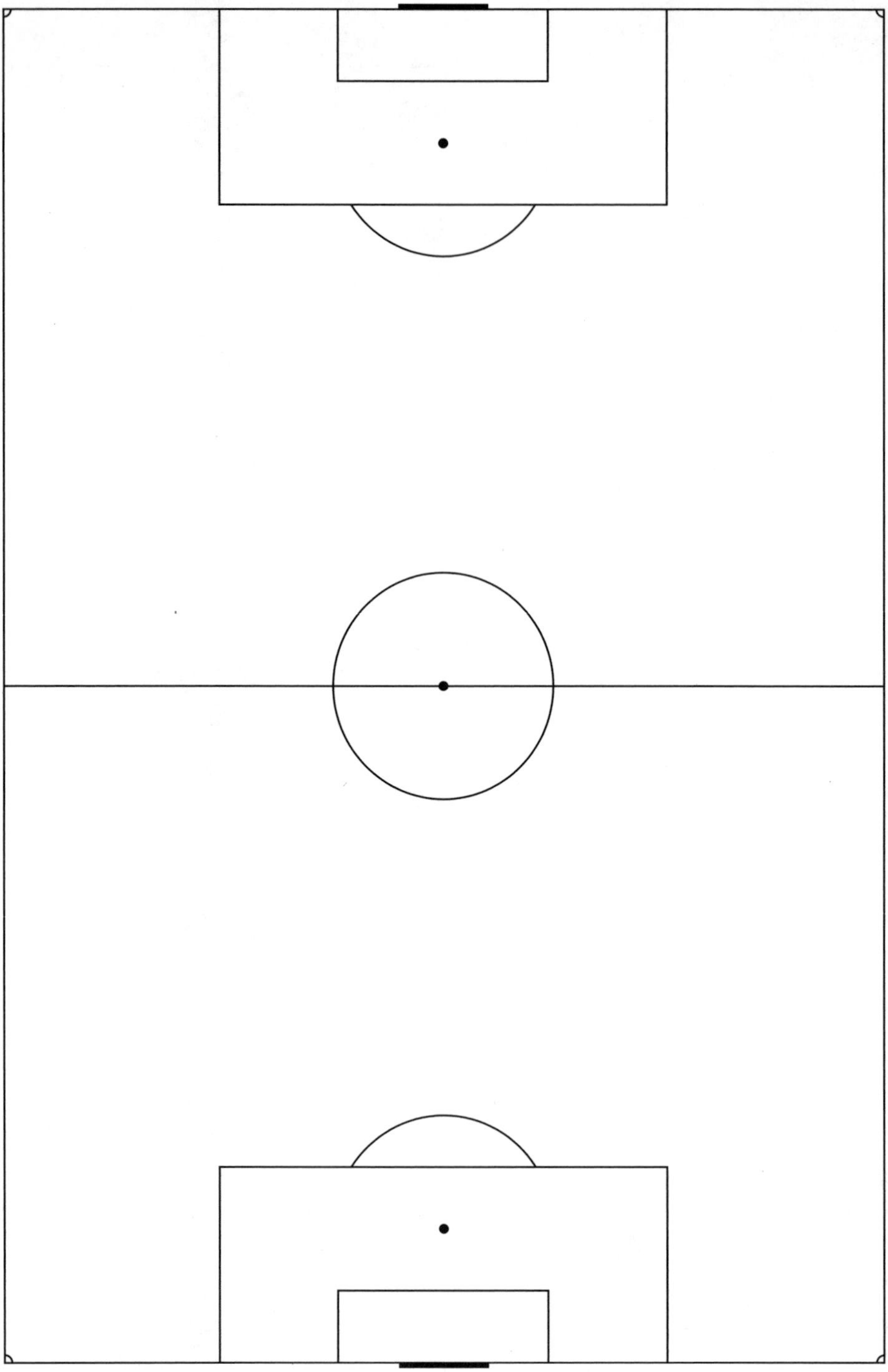